# TWELVE

# LOS ANGELES

# POETS

I0134682

The
ONTHEBUS
Poets Series
Number Two

Edited by
Jack
Grapes

BOMBSHELTER PRESS
LOS ANGELES

Bombshelter Press
http://www.bombshelterpress.com
info@bombshelterpress.com
PO Box 481266 Bicentennial Station
Los Angeles, California 90048 USA

© 2002 by Bombshelter Press.
All rights revert to authors upon publication.

Layout & Design: Alan Berman

Library of Congress Control Number: 2001 135632
ISBN: 0-941017-14-1

Printed in the United States of America

Front cover painting by James Doolin,
*Twilight,* oil on canvas, 82" x 72", 1999

Back cover painting by Lucinda Luvaas,
*L.A. Fever,* oil on canvas with sculpted
frame, 58" x 74", 1992

# CONTENTSCONTENTSCONTENTS

# SHARON DUNCAN

# ALAN FOX

# JAMES GREGORY

# JEAN KATZ

# TWELVE

# LOS ANGELES

# POETS

**R**uth Bavetta, a graduate of the University of Southern California, California State University at San Bernardino, and Claremont Graduate School, formerly taught drawing and art history at San Bernardino Valley College. She has been published in *Rattle, Spillway, The Writer, Tempo,* and *ONTHEBUS,* and her artwork has been shown nationwide. She loves the light on November afternoons, the smell of the ocean, a warm back to curl against in bed. "I hate pretense, fundamentalism, and sauerkraut. Once it was important to me to figure out who I was. Now, in my 60s, I'm content that I am who I am. All I need to know is that I am human, separate and mortal—and that's where the poetry comes from."

Photo by Leif Vogt-Nilsen

# The Water Birch

When the tiny tree first appeared,
over thirty years ago,
near the foot of the giant Douglas fir
in front of the family cabin,
my mother, the landscape designer,
and her friend Bob, the nurseryman,
studied the leaves and the growth habit
and declared it to be a water birch.

Mother is eighty-nine now,
and has forgotten the names of trees.
Bob is not much younger,
and he's buried his wife.
After my father died, we thought perhaps
Bob and Mother would get together,
but nothing came of it.

The water birch has flourished.
This year, like every year
for the last twenty-five,
it has borne a crop of little green apples.
They ripen and fall to the ground
late in the fall, long after
Mother has closed the cabin
and gone away for the winter.

# Faces

Sometimes
I see old high school friends
walking down the street,
and hurry after them only to discover
they've disappeared into someone else.

Once I spied my former college roommate
buying a baguette in Paris,

with a copy of *Le Monde*
tucked under her arm.

Then there was that freezing day
in April, 1988,
when I rode the up escalator
out of the Moscow subway,
only to catch sight of my ex-husband
going down.

It must be
that there are only so many faces
in the world,
and the longer we live,
the more familiar they become.

Just yesterday,
I came face to face
with a little man,
with thinning grey hair
and a moustache,
alone in the supermarket.

He put a single jar
of Dundee Orange Marmalade
into his empty basket,
then turned away
and pushed his cart down the aisle,

leaving me
clutching my own jar of Dundee,
and watching my father,
twelve years after his death,
disappear around the corner
toward the checkout stand.

# Reconstruction

When I sit at my desk
I can see the wall I built
beside the row of eucalyptus trees.
I used the concrete
I broke out of a section of the patio.
The day before I started,
I went to Carlsen's Hardware.
It's an old-fashioned store where the light is dim,
the stock is piled clear to the ceiling,
and they still have scoops for weighing nails,
where you're helped by old geezers in denim aprons
who know how to handyman.

I told the short, bald guy
with the pencil stub behind his ear,
that I wanted a sledgehammer.
I followed him as we snaked past the barbed wire
and the post-hole diggers,
past the stepladders and the stove bolts,
into the back room, where a row of sledgehammers
leaned against the wall.
"Who's going to use it?" He wanted to know.
"I am," I said.
He picked up the smallest and held it out to me.
I reached around him and grabbed the biggest.
"Oooo-kay," he said, with that I-know-better-
but-I'll-sell-her-what-she-wants tone in his voice.

The next morning
I hoisted that sledgehammer
and dropped it onto the concrete patio.
I split the skull of my ex-husband
and wiped the holiness off his face forever.
I cracked open his smugness.
I smashed his reasonableness.
I broke the back of his visits to my dreams

and pulverized the memory of myself
pleading with him to come home.
I cracked the head of my former father-in-law
who laughed at me
when I said a woman could be President.
I crushed that moment of misery and weakness
when I agreed with him
that education was bad for women.
I shattered the memory
of staying where I wasn't wanted
because I was afraid to leave.

I spilled the brains
of the faculty committee
who hired the young blonde instead of me.
Then I got bad John Derker in the shins
for calling me names in the fifth grade.
I gave him an even bigger one
for three years later
when he stuck his dirty hand down my blouse.
Smash for the cousins that took me to court
and the high school friend who stole my guy.
Pow for the psychiatrist who ratted on me to my ex
and pow for me for not reporting him.

The concrete cracked and split
into jagged chunks of everything I hated.
I heaved them into the wheelbarrow,
carted them across the lawn
and built a retaining wall.
Now they're just stones
and when it rains,
they hold back the dirt
from washing into my garden.

# July Morning

When I open my eyes,
I see puzzle pieces of bright blue sky
through the branches of the magnolia.
The sun glints on its polished leaves
and turns them into patches of silver.
From across the canyon
I hear the man who's building a deck.
Bang, bang, bang, goes his hammer.
Bang. . . bang.
Then it stops.

Next door,
the Labrador retriever barks once
and is answered by a thin, high yip
from several backyards away.
The wisteria vine shifts slightly
in just a breath of a breeze,
and a single lavender blossom floats,
spiraling down
to rest on the empty birdbath.
Beside me, my husband rolls over
and runs his fingers
along the curve of my hip.

# Keys

My mother is outside early this morning,
fiddling with keys.
Her legs are pale and bare
beneath her short red bathrobe,
and she's stuck her feet
into an old pair of slippers
that used to belong to my father.
As she stands in the backyard,
a finger of sun reaches through
the oak tree to touch her white hair.

Last night my husband and I
brought her back here to her house
from the family cabin.
She didn't want to stay long at the cabin this year.
"The river's no good for swimming any more,
and they've cut down so many trees.
Besides, all my friends are dead."

But there's too much to take care of
here at home—
the screen door has a broken hinge,
her favorite clippers need to be sharpened,
and the light bulb on the front porch
is burned out.
One day
she talks of leaving
and going to live in "one of those places."
The next,
she says she'd rather die.

Now she's wandering from one door
to another—the workshop,
the front door, the side door,
back to the workshop,
over to the garage apartment.

Finally, she comes into the house
and stands in the middle of the carpet
in her muddy slippers.
My husband's key chain
dangles from her fingers.
"I have all these keys," she says,
"and I can't make them fit anything."

# Buried in the Air

The sky is gray here in Geneva.
A gentle rain began about an hour ago.
I sit in a front row chair
and stare through the windows
at a mass of trees.
The funeral is entirely in French.
I don't understand a word.

It's raining harder now.
The wet leaves shine,
and water runs along the curb.
A twist of smoke
rises beyond the trees.

My brother-in-law's name
pops out of the stream of French.
I watch the smoke drift upwards.
When the congregation rises,
I stand with them.
I think we are saying the Lord's Prayer.

When we sit down again
I see great gouts of dirty smoke
shooting towards the sky.
It's not a house,
over there behind the leaves,
it's the crematorium.

At the reception afterwards,
I hold a glass of white wine
and let an old Danish man
flirt with me.

# Reflection

There's a woman with white hair
in my mirror.
She leans forward,
wets the tip of her finger,
and runs it along a dark brown eyebrow.
She dabs Erace onto an age spot,
then smoothes on the same Estée Lauder
Natural Beige makeup
she's worn for more than thirty years.

She brushes her cheeks with blush—
she knows now why old women
wear too much rouge—
then takes a Kleenex
and scrubs off some of the color.
She'll wear a bright scarf, instead.

At last, she turns from the mirror,
and I walk out of the bathroom—
a young woman,
slender,
with dark brown hair.

# The Examining Room

My husband and I sit in the examining room
waiting for the neurosurgeon.
On my lap I hold the big envelope
with the images of my brain from the MRI,

images that show the tumor, shining white
in the middle of the blacks and grays.
The walls of the room are cream-colored.
A plastic model of the spine

sits on the beige Formica counter.
Next to it lie a white towel, a tuning fork
and a little hammer for testing reflexes.
I look at my watch again.

The doctor is running late.
My husband props one foot across his knee.
If this thing kills me off, who will tell him
he shouldn't wear white socks with those shoes?

# Meningioma

I'm carrying an egg
around in my head.
I have to walk carefully
so I don't disturb it.

It sits right in front,
in the center,
an inch above my eyebrows,
cradled by the two halves of my brain,

cushioned by the rules of linear perspective,
the Principle of Uniformitarianism,
the first ten amendments to the Constitution,
and my grandmother
curling my hair around her finger.

A round white egg,
like the hard-boiled egg
baked in the middle of a meatloaf,
except this egg is raw
and I have to be careful not to break it.

On the brain scan,
I saw blood vessels
snaking down to nourish it.

Scans are black and white,
but I remember this one red.

I have to be careful
when I set down my heel,
so I don't jar my egg.
I mustn't move too fast.

When I lie on one side in bed,
or if I lean over to tie my shoelace,
or nod,
or shake my head,
I must ask its permission.

The sky is blue today and the breeze
blows cool from the coast.
From behind the high block wall,
I can hear the children next door playing.

# Mother's Day, 1964

There are fourteen of us in the photograph.
We stand in a row
in front of my grandmother's screened porch,
squinting into the California sun.

We've crowded together
to fit into the picture,
from fat Uncle Johnny on the left,
to my skinny husband on the right.

My grandmother, at ninety-one,
sits in her wheelchair,
a corsage of white gardenias
pinned to her dress.
The youngest is my son,
just over a year old.

In less than twenty years,
my three aunts, their husbands,
my grandmother, her companion,
and my father,
who's taking this picture with his new Nikon,
will all die.

Uncle Johnny will go first.
He'll stop for a beer after work,
come home complaining of indigestion,
and be dead within the hour.

My husband stands slightly apart
with his hand on my son's shoulder,
holding him apart, too.
In ten years he will sue me for custody.

I'm near the middle,
wearing a dress I've made myself
and holding my daughter's hand.
I've taken off my glasses.
Without them, I don't look like myself.
Without them,
I can hardly see where I'm going.

## Morning News

As my husband
walks towards the street,
the seat of his jeans sags
over his diminished butt.
Wispy gray hair, what's left of it,
scraggles over his collar.

Knees akimbo,
he picks up the newspaper,
frowns at it,
then looks up.

When he sees me at the window,
in my old blue bathrobe,

he tosses the paper into the air,
then flips it under his arm
like a swagger stick—jaunty.
His stride quickens.
A smile lights up his face.

## Two for a Dollar

The way they came barging through the door
was kind of scary.
They'd been lined up since six in the morning
and they were raring to go.
The couple from the day before, who swore
they were only in the neighborhood to visit
and couldn't come the next day,
were first in line.

I had thought I was going to sell Aunt Katie's things
to her friends and neighbors.
I imagined a young couple, just starting out,
measuring the dresser
to see if it would fit in the baby's room.
I wasn't ready for those people
who came piling into the house.
I wasn't ready for the woman
in the bell-bottom pants,
or the guy with the toothpick.

Steak knives with plastic handles,
two cigar boxes full of broken costume jewelry,
a pair of golden cocker spaniel bookends,
the plastic Madonna that was supposed to light up,
but didn't.
People pushed and shoved.

They tore the price tags off the dining room chairs
They opened the hall closet
and grabbed out the rug and the teapot
I didn't intend to sell.

Toenail nippers, a length of purple polyester,
the cedar chest with broken hinges,
a painted teacup and saucer from Catalina.
A fat woman who smelled of sweat and cigarettes
stood guard over the maple hutch.
The glass rooster, the chrome dinette chairs,
the apple blossom china, almost unused,
but not quite a whole set.

A tiny black-haired woman
in Calvin Klein jeans went out to the garage,
and yanked a cabinet off the wall.
Uncle Johnny's tackle box and rusty drill bits,
all his typewriter repair tools, the vacuum cleaner.
A blonde in high heels
tried to hide a lace collar inside a Bible.
Mattresses and end tables, the wheelchair,
the crucifixes from Aunt Rosalie's
and Aunt Mimi's funerals.
A dozen cans of cat food, the Silex coffeemaker,
half a box of adult diapers.
In two and a half hours
Aunt Katie was gone.

# Mileage

I'm almost out of gas
when I see the Chevron sign.
Three cars are there when I pull in,
which means I have to maneuver around
so the pump will be on the right side of the car
When I step out of the car

a gust of wind catches my hair
and blows it forward over my face.
Rain is beginning to come down in earnest.

I shove my Visa card into the slot.
The window reads "Error, insert card again,"
so I do it again.
"Band error, please pay attendant."
There's an oily wet slick
spreading over the concrete.
I walk across it as if I'm walking on pond ice,
and hand my card to a pimpled boy
in a dirty windbreaker.

Back at the car,
I remove the nozzle, lift the lever
and pull the trigger.
Nothing happens.
The numbers in the window
read, "$12.87. Thank you."
I push down the lever, then lift it again.
This time the numbers click to zero
and gas flows into the tank.

The wind blows a palm frond
across the blacktop.
A large puddle reflects red, white and blue.
I remove the nozzle,
screw on the plastic cap
and wonder what the weather
will be like ahead.

It's getting dark now,
and the rain is coming down harder.
It would be nice if I could turn back,
but I buckle myself into my seat
and pull onto the freeway.
I'm up to sixty now
and still moving forward.

**C**hiwan Choi first fell in love with writing after reading *Ham on Rye* by Charles Bukowski in 11th grade. He has been reading and writing ever since. He has published two collections of poetry/prose, *Dogfuzz on the Asscrack*, and *lo/fidelity lovesongs*, plus a number of chapbooks. He has done readings at various cafes, bookstores, and bars, and he thinks he has been permanently banned from reading in all public libraries.

# partners

there's nothing more beautiful
than watching her face
when she masturbates,
as she rubs herself,
opening her eyes to look at
her own big clit with such love,
until she cums,
her body bending and lifting
off the bed,
as she turns to me and says,
"see, i don't really need you at all."

# with all this fire we must be in hell

i've been in this neighborhood
for 21 years now.
there are faces i recognize
from fifth grade when i go to
the grocer's.
we look at each other
with what appears to be fear
trying to figure out the familiarity.

except for
the muggings
and shootings
and husbands screaming at wives
and wives screaming at children
and children screaming at the old folks
who take slow walks
in the morning,
it's a quiet and serene place
my neighborhood.

but lately
the fire trucks roar by every night

three or four of them
south down crenshaw blvd
as late as 4 a.m. or later
with sirens going
at full volume.

i am usually still awake at this hour
or i have slept and
already gotten up
but there are times when
i am sleeping
and the sirens
wake me up
and i bolt out of bed
fall down
twist my knee
and look out the window
sniff the air for smoke.

but nothing.
always nothing.
the sound of the fire trucks fade out
and i return to bed
wonder why it's still so hot
even with all the windows open.
the dog is snoring outside
beneath my window
and the other one is barking
at the fading sirens.
the barking stops too.
we are just playing pretend
as if
our lives are in danger
as if
our lives are precious enough
to be rescued in the middle of
the night.

i stare at the ceiling
until my eyes adjust to the dark.
christ
there goes the clanking of the dumb bells again.
the guy across the street lifts weights
twenty four hours a day.
i don't think he even stops to piss
he just sweats it all out.
i can't sleep.

wait.
i smell something burning.

oh.
it's just
me.

## anal sex

what sucks most about
sticking your finger in a girl's ass
is the shit that gets buried
under your fingernail.
it's hard to clean it out with a tissue
and neither of you really want
to acknowledge it.
so you keep it there for the day,
lifting it to your nose for a quick fix,
to your tongue for a taste
of this remnant of love.

## chaser

i sleep without blankets
and unclothed
on a fifteen year old mattress

and sheets stained with
blood
from a cut finger
on her left hand
and it's not really sleep
really
because my soul is
too loud
and i am afraid of
what my neighbors will
hear
at nights
from my darkness
through my open windows
surrounding
my space with the cold
that i wish will strike me
down
and these are nights
these are the nights
oh these are my nights
in a paper boat
floating on this flaming
creek of tequila
with beer
to chase the present
out of my soul
or was it the other way around
and am i backwards
dying
to reach my life.

## blades

there is a beige two-story house
up my street on bronson avenue

and before the sun
i walk to it and stand
outside in the dark holding
my two dogs by their leashes
until they grow impatient
and lick the grass blades for
the dew that quenches their thirst
and i look up at the three small windows
of the bathroom
lit
my free hand rubbing
the belly under my shirt
and watch for the person inside
sometimes a woman
sometimes clothed
getting ready for the day
of work and family
and disappointed romances
and washing her face a little
better to cleanse the broken
pieces of hope off the skin
and my mornings
each one
begin on my feet in the dark
looking for
a life
a window
a house
a second floor
a face
that is not mine
and once
it was a saturday
and the woman naked and the curtains
open stood at the window
turned toward the street
and i couldn't see her face

but she stood there for
five or six seconds
until she closed the curtains
and i walked on.
and in the afternoon
i sit in the car on beverly headed east
and my girlfriend turns
on the wrong street
and as she drives in circles
she regrets not dumping me three years ago
and her friends are telling
her that i am not the right guy
and i say, i told you to turn the fucking
car on virgil,
and we don't speak anymore through
the ride
this broken body
can't hold the sparrow
of the cactus and the lights inside
the glass
infinite and infinitely
this night
back in my bed
trying to breathe so i can see the future
but it's just channel thirty-four
and barking dogs
and the phone
and her voice
and my life
and bare breasts at a window
and her life
and she is crying
and she is crying
i know that sound
and she is crying
and what do i feel,
and do you feel anything, she says, anything

at all
and i put my right hand
inside my shorts
and think that it's already october
and what i feel
is only pain.

# ecclesiastes 4:2–3

and i declared that the dead,
who had already died,
are happier than the living,
who are still alive.
but better than both
is he who has not yet been,
who has not seen the evil
that is done under the sun.

my mother told me that
i had a little sister when
i was four years old,
but my mother's back hurt her
in the kitchen of her mother in law's house
cleaning the bone chips
from twenty-five pounds
of short ribs
squatted
with cold feet
with a butcher's cleaver
rusted
and wooden handled
and how they accepted her only
for the two sons
that she had brought into
the family lineage
my brother and i
names to be carved into

the tombstone of my dead grandfather
my name there too
third on the list
but my mother's back hurt so much
thinking about the soy sauce marinade
and the house that my father
had promised to build for her
before another sub-zero
winter
of frozen dogs
hanging stiff from the balcony
and she told me once
when i came home from wilton elementary
after asking margaret to the dance
and threw my books on the kitchen table
and opened the kinney shoes box
filled with baseball cards
a topps george brett rookie card
with rounded corners
the one with the picture of him holding
a bat on his shoulder
sitting on top of the heap
ready to run back out
the door
the sound of her sewing machine low
from her room
the taped sermons on her black cassette player
with the pause button missing
her hum too
there
downstairs in the parking lot
of the apartment
on gramercy drive
the fellas
leaning
and kicking backfoot against the fence
i could hear them

as i opened the door
and my mother
called my name
my mother
called my name
and i stopped
because
my mother
called my name
and she came outside wiping
the lint of the fabric
on her blue apron
her hair much longer then
i scratched around the scab
on my left elbow
and told her i would do my homework later
and she said
that i once had a sister
a baby sister
when i was four
the fellas kicked the fence
they sang pacman fever
they pretended they were fernando valenzuela
i scratched too close to the healing wound
she said
that her back hurt too much
and i had a baby sister
when i was four
i put george brett in my pocket
he was my lucky card
she said
i wouldn't remember
i was only four
it was a baby sister
my mother's back hurt
she said
my father eventually built her the house

a three-story house
it was haunted
i remember the ghost
i remember the woman on the stairs
i remember crying in my father's
arms
i remember that he was the only one
who could see what i saw
i was four
she said
do i remember
the ghost
the little sister
i was only four
do i remember the dead in our house
do i remember the dead of our garden
she said
her hands wiping again on
the blue apron
although they must have been clean
she said
she was my little sister
she was beautiful
she had the same small eyes as me
she had my father's downward brows
she could have been beautiful
she could have had my eyes
she could have had my father's brows
she would have been beautiful
she said
her back hurt too much
she said
i leaned back against the open door
and almost fell backward
when it swung closed
from the pressure
she said

she killed my baby sister
i was only four
i wouldn't remember
she turned around
and walked into her room
the sermon on her tape
the hum on her lips
the pain in her back
she said
do i remember the dead
do i remember the dead of our house
do i remember the dead.

## thieves like us

we talked on the phone,
each of us watching
*the bicycle thief*
on pbs in our own dark rooms
and she asked what was happening now
and i said that dad was beating
on my brother for losing his money
and she said that
this was a strange and sad movie
we were watching.

## when i'm sober

i see how beautiful
and good
my life really is,
but i can't write that way.
so i drink and drink
until i see nothing
but blood
and flesh
tearing.

# first kings 19:3–4

elijah was afraid and ran for his life.
when he came to beersheba in judah,
he left his servant there,
while he himself went
a day's journey into the desert.
he came to a broom tree,
sat down under it
and prayed that he might die.
"i have had enough, lord," he said.
"take my life."

two twenty one afternoon
meltdown
whiskey from a chinaman
and ninety degree heat
a black man knocks on a blue door
across the street
as the dogs limp upstairs
at the metropolitan museum
through the paintings of el greco.
the chirping of the bird
is loud
because it is inside
entered through open windows
to drink the water
from my skull.
the shelves are lined
with people that no longer exist
no matter how much they smile
no matter how much i love them,
raining ash
down the fireplace
the whiskey spills
on the open bible
on the prophet jeremiah
halleluiah

halleluiah
oh bring the white wolves
on chariots of opal
howl love songs
to my bones
oh bring the wings of philadelphia
dipped in the spit
of a martyr
of a whore
of a poet.
(two shots from the window
will leave a four-year-old boy
crying next to his mother
flat on her back
with a crooked knee.
i've seen it before.)
on a boat floating
through a river in a south american jungle
holding on to the edge with one hand
to a native's hand with the other
my father stood up
looking so tall
like he was something i would one day read about
and pointed out to the water
to an end i could not see
and said that i should look out there
because this is not
where we were going to be.
it was just a stop.
we are headed somewhere else.
come back to me
come back to me
bring the heart of a sparrow
in its own beak.
the perch hooked
lifted above an old soldier's shoe
the blue paint of a truck

melting in the salt.
waiting to wake up
waiting to find something
like love hanging
from your lips,
blooming flowers of four a.m.
shriveled up and dead
by noon,
on a tour bus
with fifty old men and their wives
on a four-day trip
to see the waterfalls
of her eyes.
it is easy to give up.
it is easier to pretend to be fighting.
sometimes
outside on the front yard
on my back on the grass
my head resting on my dog's back
as the other one rolls around
in the sun,
squinting at the sun
and listening to the neighbor
telling her daughter to put her
clothes back on,
my head rising and falling
to the dog's breathing
i can believe that i still
have what it takes
to get there
or that i will find what
i don't have
but this isn't often
because the words simply run out
and i know
that drinking is not
for fun or for the life of the writer

anymore.
it's not for any life at all.
it is just killing me
and today in the sun,
it is the only truth i know.

# happy days

it's so windy outside. i keep thinking i hear rain. i want to know where my happy days have gone. they just kind of picked up and left. i'm starving for them. i feel empty. i don't have anything to put inside myself. i am broke. i am broken. i remember happy days on gramercy drive where i learned to rollerskate but never really learned how to stop coming down the hill. i just jumped face first on the first piece of grass i could find. *rocky and bullwinkle* taught me english. i learned to dare from a spinning bottle in the middle of white boy scott's living room floor. i tried to make it stop and point at margaret but when i dared her to kiss the boy she like the most, she turned red and crawled over to scott and kissed him on the cheek and it didn't matter how much i hoped she'd kiss me. what was the soundtrack of that part of my life? i think it was journey, "open arms." right now it's leona naess, *comatised*. cheesy lyrics but her voice is sad and it breaks my head into pieces and i bought it used two days ago and i've now listened to it 14 times. it was mother's day this sunday. i bought her a pink mother's day swatch. it came in a plastic ball filled with plastic roses. she said she liked it. i found her sunday night by herself in the living room. she was sitting on the couch and the tv wasn't even on. but she was wearing the watch. when she saw me, she lifted her left hand so i could see it. i asked her the time. she said 9:13. and she put it on the next morning to go to work, trying to make sure that her clothes matched her pink watch with the roses on the strap. i hear music. i hear her music. it sounds like yesterday. i wish it was enough to take me back. she sat alone happy with her watch. dad was sleeping in his room. they each like to be alone. he's upset with her family. over dinner the other night, he was complaining to me. he's upset because he's take care of mom's mom for the past 17 years here in los angeles while mom's two brothers and two sisters have done nothing. but when my uncles came here on my grandfather's one year death anniversary, they told my dad that he should butt into their family matters. in the old days, dad would have taken them outside and beat the shit out of them, but he just nodded and stewed inside. and he was complaining to me about mom's crazy ingrate family and mom got pissed too and told him to just stop it. i laughed. sometimes i don's know what to do. i need to learn so much more. i'm just a child. i wonder if it happened like this for them too. the happy days. i wonder if the happy days are gone for them. the next night my dad was sitting alone in the living room on the couch and he asked me to help him. he leaned over and pushed some of his hair aside. there was a bleeding cut there. i took the pincers. i picked up a cotton ball with it. i poured some rubbing alcohol on the cotton. i leaned in closer to his head, close enough to smell the sweat from a day's work. i touched the cut with the wet cotton and cleaned his wound. he sighed. he said he couldn't sleep because he felt bad, he felt bad because he thought he hurt mom's feelings. i rubbed his head with my hand and laughed again. i said that's okay. he sighed. and the blood was dried on his cut, half an inch long from banging his head on the garage door again, and i saw a glimpse of my life on that wound on top of dad's head. i don't know if i'll ever be happy, but here i am, healing my father, and i think maybe i can hope again.

# neruda is dead

naked
nothing is as simple as the blood
in your veins
or the dust falling
from the wings of the bats
hanging
upside down from the light bulb.

naked
we are alone in the same bed
or almost
naked
sweating and smelling and waiting
for morning.

she says she can't do it
and keeps her panties on
but i slip my hand inside the fabric
and finger her anyway.
then she takes me in her mouth
and i fall asleep
while she is sucking me

and when i wake up
i don't even know that i've been sleeping.

you fucking fell asleep,
she says.

i did?

she is very upset
and i think she is going to cry.
i can't stand tears
in bed
i can't stand tears
naked
because it just doesn't fit.

you don't like me, she says.

i try to explain
that it's nothing like that
i like her
i love her, in fact
but it's been a long day
and i just needed a little nap
so i can go until sunrise.

in her skin she wonders
in my time
in ours
if things will be different or not
with eyes closed
i wonder too
why.

and in the morning
the sun does rise
but neither of us have quite made it
this far.

and i shake her until
she wakes up
and as morning comes hot
through the blinds
i stroke myself to keep a promise
and she watches
until i shoot all over my stomach
and we look
at the pool of cum on my skin
welling up inside my bellybutton
and smile
as if
something so very important
has
just happened.

**S**haron Duncan lives in Culver City, California. She is the mother of two and has worked as a housekeeper and bookkeeper. Her work has appeared in *Spillway* and *ONTHEBUS*. She has also organized readings in Los Angeles, facilitated workshops, and managed several writing classes. When asked about her life, she invokes Rilke: "I am circling around God, around the ancient tower, and I have been circling for a thousand years, and I still don't know if I am a falcon, or a storm, or a great song."

Photo by Kristin Duncan-Aghdam

# The Joiner

The first time my dad was hospitalized for manic depression was a week after my seventh birthday. When he returned home he brought an unfinished quilt that he had hand stitched together. I sat on the floor next to him and helped cut more squares to add to his quilt, until it was big enough for the bed he slept in with my mom. (When they slept together. When dads insomnia and compulsions didn't drive him to acts that would later, ironically, benefit me.)

It wasn't long though, before dad began to do odd things again. One morning I walked in the kitchen to find him standing near the sink. It smelled like ant spray, and dangling from the ceiling were cinnamon rolls. Dad had taken a package and poked yarn through each roll with a knitting needle. He used black masking tape to hold the string to the ceiling. He smiled and said, *now the ants won't get our food.* The next day my mother drove him back to the hospital in Camarillo, where he would be admitted time and again over the next several years. The drive took a couple of hours from Culver City along Sepulveda Blvd., past the Veteran's Cemetery, with its rows of white stone grave markers, through the tunnel where my brother and I would bounce on the back seat and ask mom to honk the horn of our green, convertible M.G. Then the winding road to the San Fernando Valley and west bound on the Ventura Highway. There wasn't a freeway there, then, that summer of 1955. Just a two lane highway, one lane heading west and one heading east. Both sides lined with eucalyptus trees and beyond those, strawberry fields as far as the eye could see.

We didn't get home till dusk, the three of us sunburned and tired. Mom drove us to the Hamburger Hand-Out for hamburgs that we brought home. She made some grape Kool-Aid, and for dessert we ate strawberries with powdered sugar sprinkled on them. We didn't have to take a bath because mom was so tired. We went to bed but I couldn't sleep. I went into the kitchen with cinnamon rolls still dangling from the ceiling, shapes which in the dark were no stranger than chairs or blenders. I took twine and scissors dad had left on the table and joined the legs of the kitchen chairs to the tables legs. I tied the mop to the handle of the refrigerator door then pulled the twine into the living room and wrapped it around a sofa cushion. Then I unraveled more twine and wrapped it around the front door handle. I cut the twine and took the rest of it to my bedroom where I wrapped it around my stuffed animals and dolls; then I fell asleep with the ball of twine next to me on my nightstand.

The next morning my mother must have unraveled the twine from all its objects before I woke, and threw it in the trash. That afternoon my brother rode me on the handle bars of his bike to the pet store where we bought five gold fish for a quarter. I held the plastic bag full of water and fish as he peddled home. My brother rode the bike off a curb. I dropped the bag. *You idiot*, he yelled, and we stood in the middle of the street and watched the fish flip flop on the asphalt. The plastic bag had busted open at the seam, so it was no use trying to save them, but some neighborhood kids ran into their house and brought out a pan of water. A small group of kids had gathered around us in the street, witnesses to my disgrace. The fish lay still their gills still slowly sucking at air. We scooped them up and threw them in the pan of water. I carried it to our house not even daring to cry, for fear the motion would be too much, and some might slip out. At home, I poured them in a clear mixing bowl. Some made it. Some didn't. Mom didn't seem surprised either way. I did though.

## My Mother Works

as a cocktail waitress.
My father stands in her shadow.
My brother smokes,
and I sip rum.
Our grandpa chops off the heads of chickens,
then ties their feet to the branch of a tree
and plucks the feathers.
We wash blood into the gutter.
  Burdens

of a body
    wait
in the muscle.

## There's No Telling

what was done
to my father's brain.
His body convulsing
with the crackle of electricity.
Memories wiped away.
I wonder if he even knows who I am.
Maybe that's why my baby shoes
Are tied to the handles of his suitcase.
Dangling.
No feet inside.

## Casa Chaos

Tattered curtains covered the windows.
The walls were stained with cigarette smoke
and the baby crawled on a sticky floor.
Hungry, we began to make toast.
I was maybe five,
my brother all of three.
When the toast popped up, Gene spread
it with oleo and grape jelly.
I put more bread in the toaster.

When it began to smoke and burn
I yelled for help.
Gene jumped on the table,
stuck a knife in the toaster
and drew out the bread in flames.

What did we know  of knives and toasters,
of clean diapers
and safety pins.
The baby sat
in a puddle of pee
licking jam off the toast.

## Fire on Berryman Avenue

I ride my bike toward the smoke and fire trucks
parked in front of my house.
When I skid to a stop in the driveway, a policeman asks,
"Do you live here?"
"Yes, apartment 6," I say.
"Where's your mom and dad?"

Someone else asks, "Where's your brother?"
I don't know. I drop my bike and sit on the grass.
My mouth turns down and quivers. My eyes fill with tears.
My mom and dad drive up in the car.
The police explain that someone has played with matches.

A trail of sooty footprints lead from our front door to the street.
We follow them up the driveway and into our apartment.
On the bedroom floor, soggy sheets and blankets.
In the closet, melted toy soldiers, a charred doll, and a red velvet
box with my cross inside.
My five-year-old brother, spared.
Outside, crouched behind a concrete wall, I find him—

## Ashes and Crumbs

Midday, I'm in bed.
The curtains are closed
to keep in the darkness.
He once slept here.

Now there is a plate
of nothing but crumbs,
a pack of cigarettes
and his picture.

At times I yearn for the past.
When I would hear the whistle of the Helms Bakery truck,
I'd grab a nickel and run outside.
Mr. Colgan stopped when he saw me.
My mouth watered as I stepped into his truck.
He opened a wide drawer filled with chocolate
and glazed and jelly donuts.
I asked him to open the other drawer.
It's filled with apple turnovers and lemon pies.
I never bought anything from this drawer.
I just liked looking.

The day is slipping away.
At the kitchen sink I wash
plates, forks and knives.
I think about what he said, "It's not you, it's me."
I thrust a knife in the loaf of sourdough bread,
grab a can from the refrigerator, tip it to my mouth,
pump in the whipped cream.
Turn on the lights in my bedroom.
Brush ashes and crumbs from the sheets.

# Silk Strands

Stretched out on my bed,
I look at the ceiling as a daddy longlegs
spirals down from the light fixture
and dangles over my breasts.
My house is infested with these creatures.

Although, I have had the house tented and fumigated,
these harmless spiders keep coming back.

Each night, as I get out of bed
and move my body through the door frame
and down the hallway, silk strands stick to my skin.

## Behind My Thumb

When Jim Lovell
was asked how he perceived the earth
from Apollo 8,
he said he pressed his thumb against the window
and thought;
*Everything is behind my thumb.*
*Earth.*
*America.*
*My wife.*

He was far enough away to miss the details.
Smoke rising from a forest fire.
Rain falling over an ocean.
The mud that Joe tracks onto my linoleum.
His tongue in my mouth.
My fingers undoing his belt.
A rusted can rolling over bricks.

## Giving Over

Here on the ranch the two Jack Russels are in heat.
They hump the old German Shepherd
on every part of her body.
She just lies there.
I think the old girl likes it, though.

I sit beside the pool overlooking
fifty acres of grape vines.
I take a tangerine from a blue bowl.
Maybe it's the two hits of a joint

I just had that turns me on.
The thermometer reads 107.
Juice drips down my chin,
over my nipples, and pools on my belly.

The sun sets; I grill a steak.
While it cooks,
I rub lotion over my body,
still warm after a soak in the hot tub.
I slip my arms through the sleeves of an old cotton robe,
stained and so thin
it's almost translucent against my skin.

Outdoors I look at stars,
my eyes track two satellites, and I yawn.
King Vidor built this house and died in one of the bedrooms.
In all the years of coming up here I've never slept in his room.
*Wouldn't it be nice to share this with a man?* I ask myself.
*Yes,* I answer, *but what's your point?*

At 6 a.m. the dogs bark and I jump out of bed.
A man walks toward me.
"Hi, I'm Jake, I've come to inseminate one of the heifers."
I pour a cup of coffee and add a spoonful of vanilla ice cream.
After a swim I walk up the road and see Jake in the barn.
Thick black rubber gloves cover his arms to the shoulders.
His right arm disappears inside the heifer's vagina.
"A great hand warmer during winter," he says.
Then he slaps the heifers rump; she moos.

I invite him to dinner and head back to the house.
Some cows have escaped.
Jake heads up the road with two bales of hay
in the bed of his old pick up and leads the cows
back into the pasture.
A breeze swirls the dirt around me.
After a shower I lie down for a nap.
The curtains blow like the sails of a ship
and I think of a time when I begged

a therapist to hospitalize me,
desperate for rest.

"Just a postponement of responsibilities," I said.
"A hand to stroke my hair.
Someone to teach me
to give myself over for a moment.
I've never done that,
you know.
Given myself over.
To another.
Just let it all go."

# Ripe

I met him at the marketplace in Paris.
He held a cantaloupe in the palm of his hand
and with a finger thumped the netted skin.
"How do I know if it's ripe?" he asked.
I pointed to the blossom end and said, "Here,
smell the part that was once connected to the vine.
Ripe melons smell fruity."
We walked to his apartment.
I bought a bottle of port
and some black plums.

In the kitchen he sliced open the cantaloupe
and scooped out the seeds with his fingers.
"Let's take a bath," I said.
We sat in a warm tub of water
with the cantaloupe
and the port
and the plums.
I looked good in those days.
Very good.

# They Don't Call It Crazy in Love for Nothing

We met
back when going
steady was a chain
around my neck,
a St. Christopher
dangling.

On New Year's Eve 1964,
we drink screwdrivers.
He rubs between my legs
while driving
in his father's Ford Falcon.
I bend over,
head down until orange vomit splatters
my legs and puddles on the floor
of his father's car.
I think
I could lie
with this boy
forever.
This boy who puts his tongue between my legs.

Some say
we fall in love
with our shadow.
But it is not a sin
to follow my flesh.
Even if it leads
to dark places.

# A Different Idea

I hold my father's penis in my hand
with the care I would offer
to any wounded bird.
*No,* he says.
But I assure him it's all right.
*You are sick and I am here.*
*Don't worry, I am here now.*

His piss dribbles
on my fingers.
All the blessings
of my life replicated
in this moment.
My father and I
sharing
this final
intimacy.

This little bird
carries us
beyond
our personal history,
to my own reflection,
separate
in the frame that holds his baby picture.
Reflections
of our life together,
of our life apart.

**Ian Fox** is the editor and publisher of *Rattle*, a literary magazine, and CEO of his own real estate investment company. He is a four-time graduate of the University of Southern California with a B.S. in Accounting, J.D. in Law, M.S. in Education, and an MFA in Professional Writing. His poems have appeared in literary journals including *Spillway*, *U.S.C. Anthology*, and *ONTHEBUS*. He has been to Machu Picchu (Peru), Easter Island (South Pacific), Point Barrow (Alaska), Casablanca (Morocco), St. Petersburg (Russia), Oslo (Norway), the Orkney Islands (North Atlantic Sea), San Juan Islands (Pacific Northwest), and Fresno (California). For him, poetry is more than an expression of thoughts and feelings—it's communication at ground zero.

Photo by Cecile Garcia

# God

in the form of a shopkeeper
hailed me in the Istanbul spice market
as I hurried on my way:

"Hello.
I am here.
Everything is free."

# Perfume

A poem
is like perfume—
no one needs a gallon.

# Starlight

If I do not
write myself down
I shall disappear
one day
without a trace.

If I do
write myself down
I shall disappear
one day
with a trace.

# Kindred Spirits

The Professor and I visit in his home. We share memories,
coffee, the dreams we dream.
I buy and sell real estate in California.
He researches and teaches at Duke University in North Carolina.

I lean forward to pay attention to what he has to say.
He asks me. "Are you happy? Do you have regrets?"
At lunch we explore tenure, morality, the Internet;
we talk of women, money, solitude, love, and women.

It's his birthday. I buy pizza. We watch football on TV.
His alma mater upsets mine. He laughs as loud
as I did last year. Always attentive, he assures me,
"I'm more like you than you know."

The next morning we wake at eight,
shower, he drives me to the airport.
We hug each other at the gate.
"Bye, Craig. Thanks," I say.
He says "Bye. I love you, Dad."


# Gone the Sun

The knife chops onions on the cutting board
as the refrigerator sucks heat from cold
while the white convection oven warms
our Sunday dinner of lemon chicken.

Her heels tap back and forth
across the old brick kitchen floor
while I stroke the keys of my delight
to arrange the words of my life.

We woke up late this morning,
turned back the clock—
less daylight now to save—
she read the newspaper,

I watched football on TV.
We went out, saw two movies,
asked three kids to please not talk
in the theater, and shared a diet Coke.

The orchids on the porch will be cold tonight.
We have lost another day.

# Eyelash Moon

*With appreciation to E. Regina Manfredi*

I am a man
who treasures
the eyelash moon.

Never the full moon
looming, overwhelming;
not the glowing scimitar
of a crescent moon.

In my heaven
I commune
with black holes
and the whisper
of my eyelash moon.

Maybe it's because
I often seem
almost invisible
to myself.

Maybe it's because
I feel so small
that only a thin arm
can possess me.

# Georgia on My Mind

*Artist Georgia O'Keeffe spent her final years at Sol y Sombra, a 20-acre estate set in the shadow of New Mexico's Sangre de Cristo Mountains. The library, with wood floors and a kiva-style fireplace, was once O'Keeffe's bedroom.*
     *—Real estate advertisement*

So, Georgia, it's come to this—
someone is selling your home
and name
for a lot of money.

If I spent $12.2 million
and slept in your bedroom
would I create great art?
Would I know you better than I do?

I have a home
and a bedroom with a fireplace,
but it isn't kiva-style
and my name is common,

and even if I slept in the shadow
of the Sangre de Cristo Mountains
I would not know
the winter ache in your shoulder
or your excitement
from the color blue.


# On a Lake at Four A.M.

The ship stirs
through northern light
with engines pulsing—
a maternal heartbeat.

I close my eyes
better to see
a woman I love.

I do not know
how long
I have been asleep,
or how long
I have been
awake.

# Silk Woman

The silk she loves
flows against her skin,
the white silk spun
from a cocoon of words,
spun in her dark eyes
against dark skin
which tells her who she is
and who she is not.

Am I the moth
inside her mouth
where words form
silk cocoon, dark skin
against the words of need—
I did not say love—
until which of us can tell—
I cannot—
who is the spinner
who, the moth
who, the silk?

# Everything Considered

I have trained myself
to accept the truth
that roofs leak,
paint peels,
and flesh sags—
indeed, that decline is ubiquitous.

I used to hate the loss,
the cost of it.
I once held dear
a sense of personal insult
each time a fallen branch blocked my way.

But I am older now
and no longer rage
against the universe,
filled with miracles
and ultimate despair.


# Grace

My feet tangle like twine
when I tango with my wife.
On the polished wooden floor I sway
more into other bodies than into grace.

Our coach tonight is Shirley,
an international champion.
Her face is flawless, her voice brisk,
she flows like Bridal Veil Falls in moonlight.

Her only blemish is brilliance
as she steps into my arms. We waltz
around the swirling room until at last I realize
that in my life I have, ineptly, danced with God.

# The Pearl

Each day, like an oyster,
I add another coat
to the pearl which is my life
covering an unseen grain of sand.

Touch me and feel the luster of six children,
three marriages, several college degrees,
the warmth of fear which contributes evasion,
a depth of hope in trusting myself.

There is more to a life than appearance,
weight, or time. There is less
to my life than I had wished, but
I began from a stone.

You may wear me
on your necklace or your ring
either now or long after
my pulsing flesh is gone.

# Bangkok

I sat behind my desk chatting with a client
when he began to talk about his recent visit
to Thailand. I don't know why he told me this
but I won't soon forget the emotion in his words.

*There is a forest*
*where love takes root.*
*Inhale her fragrance*
*caress her bones.*

Now I remember. I had told my client about a friend's invitation.
"Let's go to Las Vegas and hire two call girls," he had urged me.
"Do you know how a $1,000-a-night call girl
is different from a $100 hooker?"

"No, I don't."
"A $1,000-a-night call girl really loves you."

*Descend in darkness*
*disguising that scented grove*
*to salve your soul*
*within her bosky bower.*

My client said, "My first night in Bangkok
I took a taxi to the red light district.
There were girls in the windows,
like in Amsterdam, naked, partly dressed.
I paid twenty dollars for the night and met Mai Lee."
That isn't her real name. He told me her real name
but I don't remember it.

*In this copse concealing love*
*there germinates an arbor*
*of inchoate, incomprehensible,*
*incendiary ardor.*

"The room was great. Mai Lee was amazing. Not just the sex,
which was the best I ever had, but there was a bond between us,
something I've never felt before.
We were in love. She couldn't have been
more than eighteen or nineteen. She didn't even speak English."

*There is a forest*
*where love takes root.*

*Inhale her fragrance*
*caress her bones.*

"I knew I simply could not let her go. I tipped her twenty dollars
which is a fortune there. I saw her every night for a week.
I wanted to bring her home with me. We even made plans.
We made plans in sign language to get married."

*Some ramble through the desert*
*entreating passion's blister*

*but limit their unmasking to*
*a face, a square of nonessential skin.*

"I couldn't take her with me unless we got married then and there
and I wasn't quite ready for that
but I certainly wanted her to be with me
forever. I found out I could sponsor her. There was a waiting list
but I could actually get Mai Lee into the United States."

*Eden is her name*
*arousal is her ache*
*who tarries in her garden*
*is swallowed by the snake.*

"But as her sponsor
I would be financially responsible for everything.
If she drove a car and had an accident I would have to pay.
The potential liability is enormous. I still want her, of course,
but it's a little scary. I also want to retire in ten or fifteen years."

*There is a forest*
*where love takes root.*

*Inhale her fragrance*
*caress her bones.*

# Awakening

I don't often wake up my wife at 3:32 in the morning,
but I have never dreamed before that she wanted a divorce.
She has always been steadfast,
even when two weeks ago I screamed at her in our bedroom
that I would divorce her unless
she began paying more attention to me,
like saying "hello" when I came home.

But my dream told me that I had better pay more attention
to myself, that I'm still deeply afraid of being left.

I like to scare people. Now I have scared myself.
We talked about my dream 'til morning.
Before we rose she held me
against her breasts and I said, "Davine, I love you.
I'm at your mercy."

# By the Shore

Gulls and petrels plunge and vanish
into the sea whose rabid foam
swallows and feeds the birds
swallows and feeds the fish.

Frozen by careless fantasy I stare
at the space between the sky and sea.
I do not remember coming here.
I cannot imagine leaving.

I have an urge to skim the skittering froth,
impale my heart on Neptune's harpoon,
offer my heart to the tube nosed petrels,
submerge my skin in the surge and surrender.

But I never will ask another to walk
or swim in my special flow
between the sky and sea, though
I may endure for a thousand years.

I have rusted shut since the sun was fresh,
eroded since the clouds began to fill
the torrential tide which will never wash
my mouth or fill my lungs with sea.

Sacred as the rain, my barren womb
will not produce a bird or flesh. Hope
will not enter here with its raging loss.
I shall never share more with you than this.

# If

If I had the choice
I would
die
in your arms.

# Time Present

The airplane descends.
I am tired, close my eyes,
and for the first time sense my body
slipping toward the earth.

I feel beaten down by a life
which is closer now to its end than its beginning.
This weariness is normal, not a bad thing,
though now to pick up a pencil
I need a strategy—
not just a simple swoop.

In the year 2550—
just a number, isn't it?—
I will have been dead for more than 500 years.
Shakespeare hasn't been gone that long.

I smile at the thought
that I am writ large, so large,
in the library
of my own mind,
and small, so small,
in my grave
which is the earth.

# She's Gone

Lord give us a mother like, yes, my mother-in-law Jeanne
who raised her daughter to love her family and life.
No spirit can bloom without an essence to nurture the dream
but she disappeared this morning and I hope is wandering
around Sherman Oaks. Davine called the police, walked
the rainy boulevard, talked to the merchants, visited the school
where, blanched and abandoned of the exquisite leash which
lashes each surging soul to its reason, frail Jeanne last week sat
in the hollow auditorium echoing
with children who were only eight
and now I'm concerned, she is lost,
Davine says the police have been great,
checking in every hour but the rain pours down
and the evening will be colder
and the streets can be mean to a pilgrim.

Hearken to your own heart where love's treasure overflows
the limits of your flesh, to be
with your mother before she meanders
fragile and alone, lost in the interstices
of an asphalt autoed heaven
where, golly, she could be anywhere
within a radius which loosens
every hour and we never learn in school how to deal with the—
hey, let's lighten up, it's just an 82-year-old lady
whom I have avoided really seeing
for many years because I needed
for her to see me back and she couldn't. I needed the validation
of reply in her eyes, and I see Davine searching across the street.

Oh, you who want a happy ending,
rather cherish the happy kernel,
larger than any ending or beginning,
the core of your evaporating soul,
do not dribble your essence into some far-off dumpster of a day
    which may—

I digress when I feel impotent and I feel helpless to find a missing
woman who has always been cheerful to me even when she knew
or suspected she could not remember my last sentence or hers.
Go forth in the world as an aging child, go forth in the world
to find your fortune, go forth into a world of sunset truth,
growing and green with wonder, to die with a full heart and
    alone.

# Fast Poem

I do everything fast which is why I love my computer
because I can type fast, edit fast, correct fast, print fast,
which is why I like fast food when it is really fast—
seven minutes standing in line at McDonald's is why
I don't eat there any more.  That's not true, it's the crummy food
but I hate to wait which is why I rush
to get to where I'm going fast.
If I were typing now as fast as I can think then the keys would lock
and garble would be on the page and that is why
and the only reason why I slow down.
That's not true either.
I get tired.
I want to be understood.
But if you hear more than a little irritation in my voice
you are either my wife or I slowed down more than I like
to talk to you and I think you are dumb—slow equals dumb,
    doesn't it?

I know what you're thinking because I can read your mind
which is why I would rather talk to one person at a time
and I don't like what you're thinking, you're thinking that
fast is stupid because no matter how fast I live each
day I end up in the same bed and chew so fast
that I enjoy my food less than cows who chew it twice.

# Blind Pain

Raking elm leaves in our garden
I knew my father
would punish me
since I could not collect them all.

When I have sons
we will roll out sleeping bags
among the leaves
and all of us
will see the stars.

# Cinderella Midnight

When I bent over to kiss my wife
a small toad leaped out of her mouth.

"Who have you been kissing?" I asked.
She giggled so hard
four lizards slid down each leg.

So I folded the small elephant
I had brought as her anniversary present
and refused to fuck her until midnight.

# Dining Alone

Life is longing.

Family dinners
at 5:30 sharp
when we sat on red
plastic chairs,
and passed a dishtowel
around the table
from Father to Mother

to David to me.
The burned peas and carrots,
always a meat,
always a starch,
always a salad with vinegar dressing.
It wasn't all good
but it was all family
every night of the year.

Tonight I gobble
a Del Taco burrito
at a table set for one.
I sit on a yellow
plastic chair.
They got my order wrong
but I'm in a hurry.
My wife and I
and our daughters
seldom eat dinner together.
It may be the times.
It may be us.
It may be me.

Life is new.


# Quiet Times

On our first date
we sit on her sofa
and talk until three in the morning.

On our second date
we sit on her sofa again, and talk.
At midnight I say,
"Let's be quiet for awhile."

She flies into my arms.
Seven months later we are married.

She's in the hospital now.
Her mother, grown sons, and present husband
are with her.
They call to let me know
that she may die this afternoon.

I hold the phone to my ear
listening to my own breath.
I remember our quiet times
and say nothing
for a long time.

# Connection

Today my father moved his bed,
his lamps, his belts and hats—
the accumulated stuff of 60 years—
out of his home where my mother died
four months after a brain tumor was removed,
resting in the den where she had slept for eight months,
45 years before, while recovering from a slipped disc—
into a new house close to my brother and me.

Last night he told me he would never move again,
no more trash bags or cardboard boxes,
so I guess David and I will be left
to cull the artifacts of his lifetime,
except for the one-carat emerald-cut diamond engagement ring
which my father bought for $250
toward the end of the Great Depression.

One morning, between her surgery and her death
my mother wobbled out of the kitchen
and announced that she had hidden her ring
so no one could take it from her.
Some day someone may find that ring,
worth dollars, but not memories.

Tonight a stranger sleeps
in the room where I grew up.

# We Are Walking

*—After a conversation with Father Daniel Berrigan*

In Prague there were nine of us, two couples and five children
    scattered through the restaurants and shops.
I tried to structure our visit. "Time to go. We have to be there
    in fifteen minutes," I would call, over and over again.
They dallied, they needed a bathroom, they disappeared.
After a while it became a joke.
When I said, "Time to go," they said,
    "We are walking . . . we are walking."

Last weekend I visited Father Daniel Berrigan. I asked him what
    he would like to be remembered for.
He said that being remembered
was not important to him.
He told me of a great teacher he had known who taught for
    fifty-five years. Yet fewer than twenty-five people attended his
    funeral.
"The work is important," he said, "not the credit."
I imagined a gravestone in an old cemetery, with name rubbed
    clean by water and the wind.

I know each journey has no real destination,
just stops along the way.
I know there will be a time when the pyramids leave no trace.
I know there is respect in anonymity
    and no lasting profit in fame.
I know what we do each day. We are walking . . . we are walking.

**J**ames Gregory keeps his home and garden with his wife Jillian in Woodland hills, California. As a surfer, satellite builder, and poet, he notes, "I find that poetry is something that *has* to come out. I believe the anger I see in the population around me is poetry that hasn't been set free. Most people in my daily life have no idea that I am a poet."

Photo by Jillian Alexander-Gregory

# Mormon Point

Below sea level,
and I drove hard
most of the night to get here.
It's a cool dry morning
on the floor of the oven.
I don't hear crashing surf,
or birds singing,
or insect wings,
or the grit of reptile scales
against broken rock.
Just the faintest whisper of a breeze.
Any scream of anguish
would be lost on the air
over the hard salt flat
of a waterless lake bed.

If not for the sound of my breathing
and the sound of my blood,
then no sound at all.
Except for the sound
of the earth sucking under my feet
when I peed next to the van
alongside the tire.
I have been so long
without a good watering
even piss is a cause for celebration.
And when I left seed behind
on the mountain of rocks above the road,
I still hope that it can find a foothold.
Even though there is no evidence
that anything at all
could grow there.

# The Crazy Guy Next Door

Heat wave today.
95 degrees downtown.
Desert winds bring in the dust.
Everybody's eyes are itching.
I can feel the autumn heat
suck the energy out of my body.

From under the hood of his orange
1972 Datsun B-210 station wagon,
the crazy guy next door
takes a break.
He keeps telling me that he is a mechanic,
that he owned a garage.
Well, I've heard his cars,
the station wagon and an older Dodge Dart,
and they run like shit.
I would have to look hard
to find cars that run worse.
Maybe they shouldn't run at all.
Maybe that's why he is such a great mechanic.
That he can even keep them running at all
should mean something.
I wouldn't let him work on my car
but then, I'm kind of funny.

I sit and stare out the window
from my little corner
in what should be the dining room.
I have a new desk
so there's finally a place to write.
I'm looking at the sunset behind
the skyline of towers in Century City,
a dark red haze hangs in the air.

I hear him try the engine
of the orange B-210.

It sounds like it's only running on two cylinders,
real rough and the timing is off.
And between the sputters and the misfires
I'm slipping away.
I'm part of some wild dream
the crazy guy has dreamed
between the turn of a well-worn wrench,
the graying hairs of his unshaven face,
and the grease under his fingernails.

In that place I'm not here sitting on an antique chair,
bought for three dollars at a garage sale,
losing my mind in the heat,
and the red smog of twilight,
and all the old cars I drove
that just never ran quite right.
The green '65 Chrysler New Yorker.
The gray '73 Oldsmobile Delta 88.
The eggshell '65 Dodge Dart.
Finding my way home drunk from parties
on sagging suspensions
and soft brakes and tires
with the polyester plies showing through the side walls.

And when I did get pulled over for weaving,
it really was just the front end shot to hell
and as sloppy as that kiss in the flower beds
with a girl I wouldn't be caught dead with
but after about 100 free beers out of some keg
at somebody's house I didn't even know.
Just rolling around on top of the petunias,
not caring about the dirt sticking to her back
or the bugs in our hair,
never waving in the hallway afterwards
or talking between biology lab and math class.

Born and bred lower middle class
from a long line of lower middle class

written out in big letters, like a billboard,
all over the side of that rusted green '69 Opel Kadet
and the red '65 Econoline Cutaway.
Trying to make driving an old piece of shit seem cool
because it was all I could afford.

And now looking for upper middle class
just coasting through the sputters and misfires
of earning a wage,
of living in small rented apartments
and driving a puke-green '75 Volkswagen Rabbit
running on two cylinders.
Down stairs, the crazy guy slams the hood closed
on the orange Datsun.
It still runs like shit
but I think he, at least, is satisfied.

# Fish Bowl

I find the house my brother
and his girlfriend are renting.
It's a tiny white house with blue trim.
There is a small chain link fence
and a few steps leading up to the yard
with roses gone wild.
Weeds have overgrown the flowerbeds
and the grass needs mowing.

It's late in the morning
but I can tell I woke him.
He's expecting me
but still asks who it is
before he opens the door.

It's my first visit to this house.
My brother wears a pair of Levi's;
nothing else.
They hang loose around his hipbones.

He needs a shave
and his eyes are red.
The living room is tiny,
the couch and easy chair
covered with fringed tablecloths.
The place reeks of stale cigarettes,
dirty dishes and dogs.
The door into the kitchen
is hung with strings of beads.
A wooden shelf unit hides
the wall and windows
next to the front door.
Every space on the shelves is filled;
a stereo and speakers,
small potted plants,
beer steins from Germany on lace doilies,
pictures with and without frames,
nautical hardware,
other miscellaneous bric-a-brac,
all covered in a fine layer of dust.

I sink down low into the couch
so deep I can barely see my brother
over my elbow.
He slumps in the worn-out easy chair
with his feet on the floor and his legs
straight out in front of him.
He stares down to the dirty carpet.
He holds his cigarette
in his right hand,
in his left a large scallop shell.
He uses it as an ashtray.
Both of his arms rest on his thighs.

As I sit, my legs are cramped
by a large square Plexiglas fish tank
that sits on a stand
and has a plate of glass on top of it.

It doubles as a coffee table.
The only fish are a few guppies.
The bottom of the tank is as cluttered
as the shelves against the wall.
There is an abalone and other large shells,
some big lava rocks,
a cinder block and gravel,
costume jewelry, a watch, and a sailing cleat.
Across the room
four small boxes of his keepsakes
are stacked by the front door.
I've said I'll store them for him.

Looking past him I can see into the bedroom.
All I can see is two dressers
stacked on top of one another.
I imagine the bed takes up the rest of the room.

The largest guppy swims around the tank
as it tries to eat something
that is too big to fit in its mouth.
The other fish chase after it and bite off pieces as they go.
Without taking my eyes off the fish I ask,
"Is that guppy eating one of his buddies?"
"Yeah," he says. "They're little cannibalistic bastards."
"Cool."

Less than two years ago I remember
sitting on a new couch
in the house he was buying.
It had a nice yard
and a white railing around the front porch.
When I came over
his wife would answer the door
and the dogs were always out back.
He had a steady job.
There were large exotic fish in tanks
stacked against both walls of the family room.

He takes a puff of his Marlboro,
taps the ash into the shell
and blows the smoke out and up towards the ceiling.
"You want some eggs?" he asks.
"Naw."
After that we are both quiet for awhile.

The guppy has its meal
most of the way into its mouth,
but it is still too big to swallow.
The others won't give up.
They circle in front and dart in
to kiss for a scrap.

# Mileage

Another typical Southern California Christmas.
The sun is out and it's warm.
A high pressure system blows dry air across the city.
I go golfing in shorts and a tee shirt.
I play with people I've never met.
After golf I go to the gas station. I need a full tank.
Christmas means lots of driving to see relatives.
An old man is standing there by the gas pumps
in a dirty gray tweed jacket, matching cap and red scarf.
His skin looks stretched, not a wrinkle on his face.
He's shaking a paper Pepsi cup.
He groans something at me as coins rattle in his cup.
I don't have any change.
I never give money to beggars anyway.
I fill my tank to the top.
I gave the man at the register a twenty
so I have to back for my change.
It's all in dollars.
When I turn to leave, there's the old man
between me and my van.
It's Christmas Eve. I put a dollar bill in his cup.

I can't look at him. I know that dollar won't buy my salvation.
It's an insult to angels.
If somebody is keeping score,
that dollar is a black mark against me.
The old man crowds my door, forces me to look at him.
His moaning picks up to a high pitched whine.
He gestures with his arm and hand.
I look into his eyes as I start to open the door.
Here we are—Christmas in Beverly Hills.
I close the van door.
The old man shuffles away, but I can still hear him
rattle the change in his cup.
I take one last look at the pump, check the odometer.
Damn, I think, I'm losing mileage.

# Hog Canyon Massacre

The tan Jeep is stalled.
The harvested barley straw
and wild oats are dry and golden
on the steep hillsides.
It is August and the morning
is heating up fast.
We are all standing here
around the crippled vehicle,
rifles loaded and ready,
looking straight down the road
into this narrow canyon
through our binoculars and rifle scopes.
I feel the morning wind
gust against my back.

One hundred and fifty yards down the road
a small herd of wild pigs has stopped
and is looking at us.
They prick up their ears
and point their noses in the air.

They catch our scent and turn away
going up the right side of the canyon,
not giving us a shot.
They are getting away.
I see the trees to our left
moving in the wind.
I see coyote tracks
in the dirt at my feet.
The hood of the Jeep comes up.
I hear Bert curse as he tries
to find out what is wrong.

> *I try to figure out why*
> *anything I do makes sense.*
> *I am not disappointed.*
> *I know my life is good.*
> *But it makes me curious to know*
> *what I might have done differently.*

Bert tries to start the Jeep.
It cranks and cranks
but it will not start.
Five hundred yards behind us now,
I see the pigs have circled around
over the next hill
where they will come back to the road.
Bert cranks the motor over
again and again.
He stomps up and down on the pedal.
We all start to smell gas
as the last pig disappears.
Bert calls his Jeep
every name he can think of.
He and Kelly start to check the wires.
He tries it again
but it will not run.
Bob and I stay out of the way,
holding our rifles,

shuffling back and forth in the dirt
not saying a word.

We have stalled next to a graveyard of sorts
where all the old ranch trucks
have been put out to rest.
Next, they take off the air filter
and start to look there
for trouble with the carburetor.
They think it might be the float.
Bert hits on it
with the head of a ratchet
then tries to start the motor again.
A meadowlark has landed
on one of the dead trucks
and begins to sing.
The air is filled with the smell
of dried-out stalks of cut grain.

> *I wonder how my goldfish are doing*
> *back at my apartment.*
> *I can't remember*
> *if I fed them yesterday*
> *before I left.*

Finally the Jeep starts,
stalls, starts again.
Bob and I climb in the back.
Bert and Kelly put on the air filter,
close the hood.
Bert gets the Jeep turned around.
We hold on tight
as he takes off up the road.
The engine coughs
and misses the whole way.
Half a mile up the road
we come across the pigs
running as fast as they can.

They won't get off the road.
Bert swerves back and forth
to keep from hitting them.
The biggest pigs have turned
up a steep-sided draw,
leading the rest by a good margin.
Bert steers up the far side
to get ahead of them.
Then skids to a stop.
The pigs come parallel to us.
They are running uphill
thirty yards apart.
We jump out of the Jeep,
fan out along the ridge.
They don't have a chance.
They belong to us now.

The pig I decide on
is a cinnamon-colored sow.
I take a good shooting stance,
down on one knee,
and let my breath out slowly.
I center the crosshairs
on her lower front chest—
where her lungs are,
where her heart is.
I hear the report of my rifle.
The bullet, as it slams into her side
makes a loud hollow thud,
like the sound of a watermelon
being hit with a sledgehammer.

> *I wonder when my mother knew*
> *she could no longer*
> *live with my father.*
> *When did she finally give up hope*
> *that they would ever stay together.*
> *I was twelve when they divorced.*

My sow does not go down
but spins a full circle
and keeps on running.
I chamber another round,
breathe out slowly,
center the crosshairs,
hear the report.
I hear the sledgehammer.

> *My wife and I*
> *started dating at fifteen.*
> *We grew up together.*
> *We were married at twenty-one,*
> *twelve years ago.*

My sow doesn't go down.
I chamber another round—
breath, crosshairs, report, sledgehammer.
The bullet passes through her neck
and blows out her spine.
She drops like a full heavy sack
and rolls down the slope.
There is no life left in her now.

> *I wish I could understand*
> *why my wife has left me.*
> *She says she needs*
> *some time on her own*
> *to figure things out.*
> *I am so empty.*
> *I find it difficult*
> *to be alone.*

Thirty yards up the trail
the big boar Kelly has shot
is exhaling his last breath
through a hole in the side of his chest
where the blood is coming out in bubbles.
I turn and look up near

the top of the draw
as Bob squeezes off, his last shot.
Two hundred yards away
his bullet rips through
the top of his sow's back,
just in front of her rear legs.
Her blood sprays all around her
in a wide arc as she falls.

She only tries to get up once.
Then I see how she lays down and dies.

I have waited a year for this hunt.
The shooting is over in seconds.
The dead pigs are spread out
along the trail below us.
Before the wind comes up again
the air is filled with the smell of gunpowder.
The jeep starts right up now
and seems to run fine
as Bert drives into the draw
to collect the three bodies.
We take pictures
and stack the animals
over the front bumper.

All around us
the hills have gone quiet.
There is not a cloud in the sky.
The morning shadows are almost gone
and the heat of August
settles over the ranch.

> I think that back in Los Angeles
> my empty apartment is cool in the shadow
> of the big tree out front.
> By now there is a nice breeze
> starting to blow through the windows—
> into the rooms.

Before I climb back into the Jeep,
I take one more look at the dead pigs.
Blood drains from them
onto the cut gain stalks.

> *Blood drains from them*
> *onto the cut grain stalks.*

# In the Night

Tonight my brother parks
on the dirt road alongside the water.
We cast out our lines
and strap the rods to the surfboard racks
on top of the car.
With the reels in free-spool and the clickers on
we'll hear any bites that come in the dark.

In minutes my brother is asleep
in the driver's seat,
his head back and mouth open
he breathes in and out.
Every few minutes now
I hear a small fish make a splash
somewhere out in the dark.
I appreciate the quiet.
The rocks along the shore grow
as the tide drops.

The water is very still.
The lights from the power plant
across the bay
reflect paths on its surface.
I'm silent. I wait.
A bite on one of the lines will cause
the reel to cry out in the night.

Maybe I will cry out with it
before I set the hook.

My eyes get so used to the dark
that for a few minutes I begin to see
things more clearly.
Then something swims by and eats my bait.

# Facing North

My mother travels in the South.
My father has gone East, I think,
to the Aegean.
My brother fishes a trawler in the West.
I walk along the shore and reach
for my lover's hand.
The whole ocean is in my eyes,
I am at a loss for words.
I want to go home.

In my house I place
these things in a pile;
a stove, a shovel,
a bottle of water, a pillow,
a roll of toilet paper, a picture frame,
a can of gas,
a box of matches.

# Blue Chips

The steel chips turn blue
as they fly away from the cutter.
I turn my head
then look over my shoulder.
I see a black and white picture
of a girl I know who has blue eyes,
taped to the door of my red toolbox.

On top of the box is a purple greeting card
with gold trim around the border.
There is a poem,
written in Chinese calligraphy,
on the front of it.
Inside the card is a poem
written by the girl in the picture.
The last line says—
*Are you beginning to understand,*
*how it could be,*
*that I love you so?*

A chip sails over the shield,
lands on my arm just above the wrist,
hair singes and a blister forms.
I curse as I brush it off.


# Surf Fishing

The moon is full,
so bright it washes out the stars.
A light breeze ripples the water.
I think my whole life could be told
in the patterns of kelp as if reading
tea leaves in the bottom of a cup.

I start to set up my gear.
I haven't brought much.

I've learned over time
to leave excess baggage behind.
Because when it comes right down to it
a man doesn't need very much;
a bucket and a bit of good bait,
a few hooks and some flat lead weights,
needle-nose pliers and a flashlight,
a good rod and a spike to stand it in.
I don't want to make things complicated,
especially when casting out.
Standing as a wave rushes
up the slope of the shoreline,
I wait for it to top out,
not coming up, not going down.
For just a second the water stands still
and I can see my reflection in the moonlight
between the swirls of foam.
Then, it is lost forever.
I will never see myself that way again.

When the water runs back down the slope
I follow it to cast my line.
Stepping into it
I put a big arch in the rod
and send the weight and baited hook flying.
I make it look effortless,
I let the rod do all the work.
It should be a thing of beauty,
so much depends on it.
And when the weight and the hook and the bait
get as high up as they can go,
no longer rising, not yet beginning to fall,
just for a second suspended in space—
I've been told that is the edge of heaven.
Between the full moon and its reflection.
And I believe it.

I stand here with my fingers on the line
and the ocean washing around my ankles,
my feet sinking deeper into the sand
as it undermines my heels.
I feel like I've been standing here forever
waiting for a bite,
waiting for an answer,
waiting for the tide to come in.

*J*ean Katz grew up in Cedar Rapids, Iowa and Fond du Lac, Wisconsin. She and her husband, Norman, have lived in Los Angeles since 1970. She earned degrees from the University of Wisconsin, the University of Chicago, and University Associates, San Diego. She is proud to be the mother of Lisa & Dan and grandmother of Miriam, Rose, and Joshua. She facilitates organizational planning processes and gives leadership workshops for school districts and non-profit organization. In 1980 she co-founded the Very Special Arts Festival at the Los Angeles County Music Center. Her poems and essays have appeared in *ONTHEBUS, Rattle, Spillway, Writing for Your Life, The American Rabbi, The Journal of Learning Disbilities, The Journal of Career Educators,* and *FutureSearching.*

Photo by Itzik Moskovitz

# Mi Ken Neit Essen Bloomen

When I was 12
I worked in the garden with Grandma.
It was in a vacant lot a block away
from our cold-water flat
above the liquor store,
next door to the gas station.
We pulled weeds between
the green beans and cabbage,
staked up the hard green tomatoes,
sprinkled carrot seeds
in the fresh dug furrows.
I wanted to plant some flowers.
*"Bobo,"* I asked, *"far vas farflaunst du
nisht kein bloomen in dem garten?"*
"Grandma, why don't you plant
some flowers in the garden?"
*"Mi ken neit essen bloomen."*
She reached for a tiny tomato plant,
dug a hole, dropped it in,
mounded the earth around the root,
patted it down.
That was her answer to everything:
"We can't eat flowers."

Once she told me
how her mother raged
at Grandma's sister, Tante Sarah,
when Sarah embroidered
colorful flowers on a handkerchief.
Great Grandmother threw
the embroidery into the fire,
screaming, *"Mi ken neit essen bloomen."*

I just brought in flowers.
A rose for the kitchen table
placed in a crystal vase

between sugar and honey.
African violets go
to the window ledge.
A paleonopsis orchid
in the living room
is slow to open, but long in bloom.

## My Twelfth Birthday Party

When the time comes for giving presents,
I walk to a little raised stage
with a microphone and a small table
where all the presents are piled up.
I look out at my girlfriends
sitting at restaurant tables.
I admire each package, untie the ribbons,
and slowly open the books, slips, blouses,
comb and mirror, scented talcum powder.
I say a big smiling "Thank you" after each present.
When all the presents have been opened
my father drags in a large heavy package,
too tall to be a bike, too bulky to be clothing.
I untie the bright red bow on top,
tear off the wrappings,
and find a bathroom scale,
the kind they have in doctors' offices.
I look at the weight lines, 10-20-30-40-50 . . . .
I look at my classmates
who are trying to suppress tittering laughs.
I look down at my body—
I see the fat belly, budding breasts,
thick arms and fingers.
I look back at the scale,
then at my overweight father,
and turn again to my guests.
I grit my teeth, smile, and say,

"Thank you for coming to the party.
  Thank you for bringing me the nice presents."
I turn off the mike.
As my father eats
the last frosting from his plate,
I walk off the stage and sit down.


# Good Girl

Mother had told me about sex,
the pain,
the demands,
the duty,
the messy wetness,
the babies,
never the beauty,
the sweet warmth,
the passion.
When I got ready to marry
I went to the doctor for a check-up.
He put me on the scale,
measured my height and weight,
took my blood pressure,
drew some blood from my arm.
He told me, "The hymen
should be broken before marriage.
Then the beginning of marriage
won't be so painful."

I did what I was told.
I walked from our flat on Main Street
past the drunks in front of the tavern,
past the county courthouse, bank,
department store, and Montrose Hotel,
up the stairs into the red brick hospital.
Mother walked beside me.

Her face had a long, worried expression.
A nurse took us to a small bare room
with a standard examining table.
The doctor told Mother to wait outside.
I lay down on the table,
put my feet up in the cold stirrups.
I spread my knees wide,
showing my private place
to a stranger for the first time.
The nurse stood beside the doctor
as he broke the hymen
with a small sharp instrument.
The nurse helped me to sit up.
She gave me a pad
to wear in case of bleeding.
I walked home with Mother,
a good girl,
ready for marriage.

## A Different Poem

One arm is flung
across my waist.
The other rests
on my thigh.
I'm awake,
press my back
into his soft, warm
chest and stomach,
our thighs entangle
as we breathe in unison,
the sleepy rhythm of the morning,
a stirring in my loins,
my morning fire.
I remember how the babies,
sucking at my breast,

awakened that same stirring.
I'd put the babes to sleep
and wait till his fire came.
Now, again, I have to wait
for the familiar caress,
the sensouous touch,
the rediscovery of
our own rhythms;
timing, peaking, sighing,
as we return to
sweet, easy breathing.
Why do they call it fucking?
Harsh word for sweet coupling,
blood and flesh, breath and fire.
Once I sat beside a man
I was beginning to love.
His arm rested,
on my shoulders.
His voice was amorous, mellifluous, low.
"I want to fuck you," he said.
I had wanted to make love with him.
If he had wanted to make love with me,
or I had wanted to fuck him,
this would be a different poem.

# Life Study

The nurse tells me to sit in the waiting room.
She has to prepare my husband for the angiogram,
maybe angioplasty for the sixth time.
I kiss him at the door of the catheter lab,
walk down the long corridor to the waiting room.
The dawn sun lights the buildings outside,
blinding me as I look at the reflection in a window.
I won't stay here.

I have been memorizing Norm,
every pore and ridge; soft belly, hard ribs,
the soapy scent of him after a shower and shave.
A shower can change how he feels about anything.
He believes in showers as some men believe in God.
If I were Picasso I would draw Norm all in triangles,
his nose, the lift at the top of his lips,
even his eyes, the point at the top of each brow
and the two points beside the cleft of his chin.
No, triangles won't work.
His ears are pure curve, wider on top,
a small upward curve at the bottom.
And his hair, what is left of it,
still curls up at the back of his neck.
I comb and caress all the curls
of his body hair with my fingers.

Nine months ago I stood in a hospital emergency room,
watched the green line of Norm's heart monitor
swing up and down, erratic,
then stop, then start with a blip,
then stop, then start again with a spike.
The nurse pulled me into the waiting room.
When I checked the door, it was locked
so I couldn't return to the emergency room.
She returned five minutes later to say,
"He's alive now.
He gave us quite a scare.
You can see him in a half-hour."

This time I go for a walk,
remembering the triangles of his face,
the feel of the hair on his chest,
wondering how to make sense
of the green pattern on the monitor,
what the doctor will say when I get back.

# Radio

Once, only radio
brought me the world,
On Sunday nights I listened
to Jack Benny and Fred Allen.
On weekdays I'd listen to
my Dad's early morning show
as he played country music for the farmers,
inviting them to come
buy bargains from his store.
His Polish-Yiddish accent
and 1930s country music.
"Dat vas Henk Villiams,
und now  kahms
Spike Jones und de City Slickers."

What fun to play
on the radio waves!
What fun to have your say
with no back-talk!
Laughter and honor and customers coming.
"Yager's moofed ahp
tsu bring prices dahn.
Vork shirts cost only
tree dollahs dis veek."
The cash register clicked and clanged
louder than the chatter of customers
buying their socks.
The second story store
with bargains galore.
The merchant showman,
microphone in hand,
making you smile.

The Iowa farmers must have chuckled
to hear that Polish-Yiddish-English wit
while they  shaved and ate their pancakes

before milking the cows
and planting the corn.

# The Fall

My daughter sleeps, a hand under her cheek on the pillow, thick dark eyebrows, ringlets of dark brown curls above her forehead, the softest sound of breath, almost a snore. I've watched that face since she was born, almost 40 years ago. Now she waits for the call to adopt her baby girl. I think about her as a mother, about me as her mother, about my mother.

My mother never watched me sleep when I was 40. By then I was watching her, catching her when she fell ill and went mad. I wish I could bring Mom back to this room, to be with us, just to be, easy. It was never easy.

I remember a day when I knocked on Mother's door. There was no answer. I called, "Mom, Mom." No answer. I rattled the door. No answer. Reaching into my purse, I found my key, turned open the lock, turned the knob, pushed open the door, and walked into her apartment. It had a burnt potato smell. In the kitchen I turned off the stove and called, "Mom, Mom," again. No answer. When I walked into her bedroom I saw her lying on the floor, breathing softly, the rise and fall of shoulders with each breath, a little blood on the carpet where she lay. Touching her shoulder, I said, "Mom" in a soft voice.

She stirred, opened her eyes, sat up, and said, "Jeannie, why are you here?" I told her about the locked door, the burnt potato pan, the stove still lit. "How did you fall, Mom? Why didn't you answer my call? Where did this blood come from?" I asked. She said, "The rug slipped. I think I hurt my arm." Her wrist and hand were turned and crooked, with a red swelling at the joint. "Does it hurt?" I asked as I touched it. "Yes," she said.

"Mom, we have to go to the hospital to have a doctor look at it."
"No! No hospital! No doctor!" "Mom," I said, "we have to. It may
be broken."

Somehow I guided her into my car and drove her to the hospital
emergency entrance. The attendant at the the counter took down
the information. He said, "We'll get you set up for x-ray as soon as
possible." She screamed, "No!. No x-ray! I won't!" The attendant
looked at me. He said, "Are you her legal guardian?" I said "No."
He said, "You will have to take her home. We can't touch her
without her permission."

I drove her home, helped her out of the car, into her apartment,
into bed. I made sure the stove was turned off. "I'll call you in the
morning," I said. After driving home, I parked my car in the garage,
walked up the stairs, into the house, found my journal between the
cookbooks, and sat down at the kitchen table to write "Mother Says
No to Everything."

# Out of Reach

I don't want to grow old like my mother,
I can see her the day I drove
to Wisconsin to get her out of jail.
The jail was clean and new.
She was the only woman prisoner.
The attendant met me at the entrance,
took me by the elbow,
guided me to Mother's cell,
explained that Mother's downstairs neighbors
called the police about water
leaking through the ceiling.
When they went up to investigate
they found her naked and chanting.
All of her possessions were
heaped in the living room,
water overflowed the bathtub,

soaked through the floor,
and leaked into the store downstairs.
The police took her to jail
until they could find her next of kin
to put her in a hospital.

I looked through the steel bars
of the cell at the brown tile floor
and brown tile walls,
a cot in the room
and one light bulb
with a circular tin shade,
all so clean.
Mother wore a brown, dirty bathrobe.
It hung open to show
her pubic hair and sagging breasts.
Her ribs showed through her skin.
Her feet were in ragged, scuffed slippers.
She paced up and down,
chanting in her cell,
"6-7-8-9," she said… "5-4-3-2   12-13-14-15."
Her eyes flickered.
Perhaps she recognized me.

I put my hand through the bars
to close the front of her bathrobe.
She moved out of reach.
"Mama," I asked, "what happened?"
"7-8-9-10," she answered,   "3-4-5-6."

# Hineni—Here I am

Joshua calls, *Grandma Jean,*
*Where are you?*
*Here I am* I answer. *Where are you?*
*I here*, he calls back. *I Josh.*

I learn from him
about the mystery
of God and our prayers.
God calls, *Abraham!*
*Hineni—Here I am*, Abraham answers,
totally present,
ready to respond and obey,
as I am when Joshua calls.

*Grandma Jean, sit down right there,*
Joshua commands.
I sit down.
*I play with animals,* he announces.
He picks up a toy lion
and places it on the table,
then a tiger and a giraffe.

*Shema Yisroael,* God tells us.
*Listen up, you people.*
*Adonai Elohenu.*
*I am The Lord.*
*Adonai ehod.*
*And I am one.*
*Pay attention.*
*I am everything*
*and I am One.*

I reach to move the lion
to the other side of the table.
*No* says Joshua.
*Lion right there!*
I listen, I hear,
and I draw my hand back.

# Three Ropes of Challa Dough

When my daughter, Lisa,
was three days old
I went to the kitchen
to bake challa.
I wanted something
rising again in the oven.
I sifted flour, salt, and sugar,
started the yeast in warm water,
mixed the eggs, oil, and yeast
in the center of the flour,
kneaded it all
until it came alive
in my hands,
let it rise,
then rolled three ropes of dough
to braid into challa
for Sabbath dinner.
It rose with its own life inside
from the life-giving yeast.
I baked the bread
until it was crusty and golden
on the outside,
soft and delicious on the inside.

Like my granddaughter, Miriam,
tough and sweet,
with intertwining strengths:
her Chinese birth parents,
her Jewish Momma Lisa,
her Christian Momma Sharon,
her own life force,
all of it,
mixed and kneaded,
rising like bread dough,
growing to become
an American woman
for the new Millennium.

# Cooking Chicken Soup

I'm cooking chicken soup again,
chopping carrots,
slicing celery and onions,
peeling skin off the
chicken breasts and thighs,
covering the chicken with quarts of water,
sprinkling in salt and pepper,
adding parsley.

I wonder if cooking chicken soup
is a form of prayer?
I wonder why I feel this urgency
to cook all the almost forgotten flavors,
to fill the house with
the aroma of soup, kugels,
kneidlach, tsimmes and borscht?

The urgency doesn't connect
with real memories.
My childhood holidays
were not so special.
The same newspaper tablecloth
covered the table as on weekdays
to save on laundry.
Candles were lit
on the back of a cake pan
to save from polishing
the brass candlesticks.
Chicken soup was an everyday food.
Guests were never invited.

At work my desk is piled high with papers,
getting ready for a conference.
I should keep working.
But a voice shouts in my ear,
"Close it up! Go home!

Prepare chicken soup and kneidlach,
kugels and borscht, tsimmes and teiglach!
Invite guests!"

In the synagogue
I carry on a silent argument
with the God of broken promises,
"How can I pray to You who permitted
the burning of Your children,
their ashes scattered across
the wheat and potato fields of Europe?

You, who are called Father
in my prayer book,
were no father to my father's
murdered brothers and sisters,
no father to the children
of Tereisen or Maalot.
We should prosecute You
in court for child abuse.
I cannot pray in the words
of this prayer book.
Only in the melodies,
only in the swaying, chanting community."

Connection is the core of my spirituality,
connection with my known and unknown past,
with the mysterious creative force,
with some eternal and unifying source,
evoked by the aroma of chicken soup.

Some voice, some spiritual voice,
whispered to me all week,
shouted at me all day,
"Cook chicken soup, Jean,
kugels and kneidlach,
tsimmes and borscht.
Invite guests."

# Young as Ever

It's time to grow a soul,
deeper than the creases on my face.
A friend says,
"As the creases deepen
the vision blurs,
so we stay
as young as ever,"
but young as ever
is not my goal.
The years are writing
poems on my face.


# Counting Backwards

Let's see,
if I have to be there at 5:15,
I should leave here at 4:15,
so I must stop and dress by 3:15,
and, before that,
I need to pick up my dress
at the cleaners,
so I can only do one more project.
Let's see,
with a little luck I may live till 91,
so I should buy the plot by 90,
clean out everything
I want to give away by 85,
write 5 books by 80,
read all the great writers and poets by 70.
Meanwhile, I've got to
walk 4 miles every day,
work for 8 hours,
drive the freeways for 2 hours
water the plants,

hug Norm 12 times a day,
cook breakfast and dinner,
answer the mail,
throw out the catalogues,
and pay the bills.
Only 2 years left
to read the great books.

I add a line
to the bottom
of my To Do list:
Live to 97.

# Wayne Liebman

After graduating from Yale University and UCLA School of Medicine, Wayne completed his residency in Anesthesiology at UCLA and has since been practicing privately in Los Angeles. An interest in ritual and mythology led him to write his first book, *Tending the Fire: The Ritual Men's Group* (Ally Press, 1991), which was anthologized in In *the Company of Others: Making Community in the Modern World* (Claude Whitmyer ed., Tarcher, 1993). Wayne's poetry and prose have appeared in *Rattle, The Sun, The Poetry Calendar, Next, Spillway, Pearl,* and *ONTHEBUS,* and in the anthology *Beyond the Valley of the Contemporary Poets* (Sacred Beverage Press, 1998 and 2000). He co-edited (with Jo Scott) an anthology of poems, *Raising the Roof* (Bombshelter, 1999), for Habitat for Humanity, Riverside. His children's plays have been produced at UCLA by the Virginia Avenue Project. His poetry was nominated for a Pushcart Prize in 2001.

Photo by J. Michael Adams

# Chimes

An infant
playing in its crib puts
the teddy bear in its mouth,
reaches for the new chimes
turning overhead, fills
the diaper, is changed,
writes in its journal:
"Day forty-nine. Suspect
the bear is not edible.
Game with mother again.
Invent music."

# The San Jacinto Hotel

The San Jacinto Hotel has eight rooms,
one TV, swimming pool, a dining nook.
Across the street, Mt. San Jacinto.
Three girls from Los Angeles
arrived yesterday. Noses painted
with white cream, they collect sugar packets
from the tables after breakfast.

This afternoon their mother takes them
to the magic shop on Palm Canyon,
where they learn to make the red ball
disappear from the cup.
Hold it in your hand, they say:
it's a real ball.
They can make it disappear.

Their mother is beautiful,
with long legs like Hedy Lamarr's.
Alone in the bedroom,
she paints her face with rouge,
sings "Dear Mr. Gable" the mirror.

Ten o'clock. The girls, in nightgowns,
sneak out. They want a look
at desert stars, the Milky Way.
They dance around the pool,
pour sugar on the ground,
watch how it glitters—
magic, they say:
in the morning, it turns to snow.

# Second Wish

You know how you lay
yourself down in the back porch
hammock, sleep all day and
wake up thinking: am I still married?
Those kids of Judy's—are they grown
yet? Is that model rocket still
in the basement—the five fins
that took all the glue?
It's the same in those stories
where the girl has to sweep the ashes
from the fire for seven days,
until the dark man lets her go—
only it could be seven years,
or seven decades in your life until
the lock springs open. And now
grown-up with gold in your pocket,
you stride into the breezy afternoon.

Isn't that the way of things—
dropping breadcrumbs faithfully,
so sure and full of hope,
then looking back and the crows
already making off with them.
You could be anyone thinking
these thoughts.
You could have wandered

into this life by mistake and still
be on the second wish, or run
any time to the edge of the forest,
calling out for the red-haired man
to take you back to the palace
where the King and Queen
remain with their son or daughter,
the feast set out, silver
glinting in the torchlight, honeyed
pears and apples from Damascus,
everyone silent as the drawbridge
clinks lower, waiting for your sword
on the iron door.

## Monopoly

We set the board
on the folding table
and divide up the play money,
wrinkled from overuse.
All around the house
the sound of rain
seeps in the walls
and spatters the windows,
left open a crack
to let in the damp,
gray-green world.
My cousin Rita, thirteen,
always wins.
She chooses
the silver roadster for herself,
the iron for me,
and sets them on Go.
Fifteen years from now
she and her infant son
will glide off a slick,

Nevada highway
and disappear forever
into a gorge.
She lays the stack
of orange cards
on Chance.
I raise the dice
in my cupped hands
and rattle the air.
*You have to buy*
*everything you land on,* she says.
*Everything.*
*It's only play money.*
I throw the dice,
advance to Reading Railroad
and count out two hundred dollars.

# Tom Sawyer's Island, 1961

I think we're played out,
up the creek without a paddle,
lost. But we move on.
My father first—ears cocked,
green eyes wide. He's serious
even when joking.
We're up Injun Joe's cave,
Tom Sawyer's Island, 1961.
Walls damp, breath in front of us.
My father plays a game.
"Everything," he says,
"comes from the ground."
"What about our house?"
"Made of wood. Wood from trees.
Trees from the ground."
He squints down a passageway,
takes my hand. His nails,

manicured yesterday at Oakley's
barber shop, reflect the lamps.
No danger here.
Each side tunnel doubles
back to the main. In Injun Joe's
cave, all ways are one;
every chance is right.
I don't know this.

Other boys pass by;
they go left, right, straight;
voices trail off. We're alone.
Somewhere, water dripping.
The wheeze of a bat.
My father hunkers down,
measures the dark.
"Wind coming from over there," he says.
He straightens, pushes forward;
leads us into day.

# ∫mudged

After a fight with my mother,
my dad took me to Disneyland.
Another time he took me to see
*The Ten Commandments*.
We went fishing on the pier a couple of times,
and boating at MacArthur park.
I always was a commodore.

He was the one who did the punishing,
who chased me into my room.
One evening my parents went out.
I sneaked into the den
where their chalk portraits
stared at each other on the wall.
They weren't framed yet.

I climbed a stool,
ran my left hand down his face
and thought, "I love her more than you."

Six months later his heart stopped.
Long after he was gone
I could see the shape of my fingers
under the glass.

# Movements

*for Suzanne Farrell*

## I. Barre

She is wise now, approaching the age he was in 1960 when they first met. She, a girl of sixteen fresh from ballet school in the Midwest, arrived with her mother in New York because New York was the center of dance, and she wanted to be a dancer. He, the émigré Russian genius, inventor of modern ballet, father of choreography, founder of the New York City Ballet company. She was tall, shy and at first Balanchine didn't single her out. But she was a quick study. An older, principal dancer, a man she idolized when she was a little girl, had seen her performing at the edge of the corps, not even visible to the audience, throwing her life into her dance, and took her under his wing. He was slated to dance in the premiere of a Stravinsky-scored ballet, *Movements*. When his partner got pregnant, he told Balanchine that Suzanne could take her place. "Fine," said Mr. B, who didn't believe it. They rehearsed in a living room, Balanchine staying away. When they opened, she again threw herself into the music, surrendered her life to dance. Stravinsky, who was present, asked Balanchine in wonder, "Who is this girl?" Balanchine answered, "She is just born."

## II. Pas de Deux

It was the sudden shiver of beauty revealing itself, a moment Balanchine later choreographed for her: a man lost in shadow, face covered in his palms; the young girl in white pulling his hands from his eyes. I was twelve and had her picture cut out of the paper on my bedroom wall; she was a piece of the sun, and I knew the sugary slope on which Balanchine now walked. He had a habit of marrying his ballerinas, was married to one then, a dancer whose career polio had ended six years before. Now he began to teach Suzanne: the quick *Tandu*, the off-balance move, the loosening and stretching of line. She was pliant, she was air, she was faith itself. She absorbed him as a child absorbs its mother and he began to create ballets for her. After rehearsals they would walk arm-in-arm from the studio, stop at the Tip Toe restaurant up 79th street for dinner, drenched in each other, consort and muse. "When you believe as I did," she later said, "You are not yourself anymore; you are your work." Their bargain was simple; she gave him her spirit; he gave her dance.

## III. Pas de Trois

When he touched her in the rehearsal hall her whole body shimmered; his fingertips blistered. She wouldn't sleep with him—because she was Catholic, because he couldn't leave his paralytic wife, because she was afraid of losing herself, because she knew she was already lost. They went on this way for seven years, loving, wounding, working, giving themselves to a kind of death where death was art, until finally, in desperation, she tore herself from him and married another dancer in the company. Balanchine, wild with grief, exiled them both—the angel of the Lord at the gates of Eden. The couple danced four years with the Bejart Ballet in Europe; home was a hotel room with a double bed. The wise and generous Mr. Bejart knew she was only on loan. In the end she wrote to Balanchine asking to dance for him again. What sweet torment her letter must have brought. He took her back, though not her husband. She danced for Mr. B. another eight years, until he died in 1983. He had made over twenty ballets for her. She went on dancing them four years more, never the same way twice, until her legs gave out.

## IV. Reprise

Once at dinner, after she returned from Europe, he came as close as he could to asking forgiveness. "It was wrong of me," he said, "The difference in our ages was too great," But it wasn't that, and she knew it. What was their choice but to plunge on? She was stricken at his death, and as she looks into the camera now, I can see grief in her eyes, and in the lines of her lovely, aging face. I want to smooth the lines, to mend them. The other girls and women of the company envied her power over him, but I think it was the power of music that catapulted both of them. The way she abandoned herself and called out his gift to make a form. She was the instrument begging to be played. And when she teaches now she feels him in every step, her body still keeping faith. "No one ever understood me, or loved me, or used me in the way he did," she says. "I have no regrets, no *if only's* in my life."

I long to give myself to something, anything, with that intensity. To believe and burn in its holiness, even five minutes.


# Captivity

*In 538 B.C., after a half-century of exile, the Jewish population of Babylon*
*was granted permission to return to their homeland to rebuild their Temple.*

I don't want to leave this place.
The gardens of Babylon are beautiful
and its gods have been kind.
There is nothing in Zion—
no Solomon, no Temple, no houses—
only the nomads we will have to fight
for scraps of bitter desert and salt air.
Here the river is around us,
the houses full of spices.

Daylilies sprout in the orchard
where we carved our names.

Tonight we will lie among the rushes.
Our wedding cake has swirls of flowers,
green and purple—we can put them in our mouths.
I want a cake as large as the moon,
full of dates and raisins, and moonish leaves.
My eyes are wide behind the veil.
Love, do not be angry.
They whisper a country of words,
a heartache blown across the waste.
What will come of us?
We will blow like weeds across that emptiness
for a god who never paid us mind,
whose laws we have forgotten,
whose name we can't even say.

# Blonde

Then I came to a part
in the book I'm reading
about the Warsaw Ghetto
where it says, *blonde,*
*whether natural or dyed.*
Referring to Jewish women
in the Resistance and
their hair. How it became blonde
if it wasn't blonde already.
And also in the book,
*when caught, they were shot.*

Women were couriers of choice
for small arms, false papers, food.
Because, when stripped,
you couldn't tell the difference
between women. Whereas,

any man without pants,
you knew: Jew or not.
That was the test for a man
suspected of criminal intent:
pull down the pants—

which was no good with women.
Who, as extra insurance,
were also *blonde,*
*whether natural or dyed.*
Otherwise, hair didn't matter.
Glamour, a memory.
Though how love,
with every safe passage,
must have grown more furious
in dark corners.
A tearing of clothes,
a glory in nakedness.
Even in the bunkers—
so temporary a home.

# White Out

The moment before
the cloud settles on me
and everything turns white,
I look back
on the familiar world,
the path that leads
up the mountain,
the line of treetops
to the disappearing
ridge,
and think
that it's possible
to turn back.
Or, worse come to worst,

I'll wait right here:
I tell myself
it's all a painting,
a dress rehearsal,
a first draft.

# City of Exiles

I think of those graves,
one for each grandparent,
the expansive granite markers
with Hebrew and English letters—
*Ruchel beth Nucham*
*Wolf ben Yusif—*
in block eighteen
section C
of the Mount Hebron Cemetary
in Flushing, New York,
last resting place
of the Carpathian Mountain village
Istitchka, on the Dniester River,
Ukraine.

You see them
from the Van Wyck Expressway:
millions of headstones
dotting western Long Island,
huge granite cities,
the old world's gift of children
to the new—
cities of the golden door.

I was told Ruchel held me once
when I was a year old.
Wolf, for whom I am named,
died before I was born.
The few pictures I have

show him toothy and thin,
her fat and dour.
She was his second wife.
The six children are gone.
The clothing store on Grand Street is gone.
A dozen of fifteen grandchildren remain.
The number of great-grandchildren is fixed at twenty-seven.
Twenty great-great-grandchildren have been born.
But I don't think of them as I stand
for the first time at the graves
in the light summer shower
saying Kaddish.
I am forty-eight and think of the old ones—
parents of Wolf and Ruchel,
who stayed back—
and their parents,
whose names and languages
I do not know.

The headstones are orange,
brighter than the trunks of the trees,
so lovely I photograph them
for my cousins and aunts.
How readable their letters are,
crisp and lovely after fifty years,
their purpose, I am seeing,
not so much to mark the graves
as to say the names—
*Ruchel beth Nucham*
*Wolf ben Yusif—*
to speak them willingly
in the living air.

# Dream of the Common Life

I have had the most wonderful dream.
My neighbor is playing a flute in the backyard.
I don't even like my neighbor.
You wouldn't either if you knew him.

All the hedges are cut down; I can see everything.
Right there in the yard: goats;
some men in skullcaps praying;
candelabra in the garage
throwing off yellow light.

They are just concluding the service.
I realize this happens every morning.
Somehow it escaped me all these years.
I've been getting up too late.

The houses are smaller and closer together,
blending over time, cliff-dwellers.
You can hand a cup of sugar from house to house.
There is no room for my boxes anymore,
the ones labeled *spells*, *rainy days*, and *reasons for things*.
This doesn't bother me, although

nothing in my life justifies such a dream.
It belongs to someone I don't know,
into whose head I've wandered by accident.
He builds a house of forgiveness.
Patience is his backyard.

**C**andace Moore attended CUNY and UCLA, studying literature, psychology, writing and comparative religions. Most recently, she worked for the Simon Wiesenthal Center, writing news stories and press releases. She and her writing partner have just completed a novel based on their seven-year experience in a dream workshop together, entitled *The Dream Sisters*. Her published poems have appeared in *Spillway*, *Rattle*, and *ONTHEBUS*, and a personal essay appears in a book on Japanese therapies, entitled *Quiet Waters*, *Flowing Bridges*. She currently lives in Southern California, where she teaches yoga and writes. She has one daughter, Shannon, who is an old soul and her best friend. She dedicates these poems to her mother, Lila, and her father, William.

Photo by Michel Lev-Pierre

# Given Circumstances

My mother is slipping away.
She dreams about mobs surrounding her,
while by day she outwits terrorists circling the hospital.
Terrorists, who pummel cyanide into powder,
and then boil it into a tasteless, odorless liquid,
which is then injected into her food and water supply.
I feel she is passing into another kind of death.

When I walk into her room,
she looks startled,
as if a cold hand had just slapped her face.
She sits with her arms crossed, negotiation-style.
The room smells of urine.
Overcooked vegetables remain on her dinner plate.
Three orange sunflowers, dyed for Halloween,
dangle from a milk carton.

She grills me to see if I am friend or foe,
not sure if I've changed allegiance,
or if I've been blackmailed.
I audition for my mother—let her know I'm on her side,
and will call the police on her behalf.
As I speak, her eyes scan the room.
She is wearing silk pajamas from Victoria's Secret
that I gave her last Christmas.
The violet-blue silk seems out of place,
not the right outfit for fighting terrorists.
The delicate anklet I gave her
clings to her ankle now, a tracking device for endangered species.

She says, "Call Robert. Tell him the terrorists are surrounding the
    hospital,
that his phone is tapped and they're trying to poison me."
I walk my mother to the pay phone by the day room,
where an orderly brushes a patient's long and tangled hair.
Mary interrupts her call to the governor
to sit for pink curlers and a new do.

"Anything else I should tell Robert?" I ask.
I notice the piano no one ever plays,
a giant music box that one day just stopped in the middle of a
    song.
Nurses circulate with dixie cups of tranquilizers and
    anti-depressants,
pills with names like Latvian cities, trilaphon, desamorpramin.

"Tell him to hurry," my mother says, "they've already killed a lot
    of people,
and they're going to kill me next."
"Robert, hurry," I say. 'They've killed a lot of people."

"The trick-or-treaters will find poison candy bars in their bags,
the bad men take hypodermic needles filled with cyanide
and inject it into the candy," she says.
She grips the TV remote control from the day room,
which has now become her cell phone.

Later that night, when I get home,
where I live alone,
I have one message on my answering machine.
It's from me, asking Robert for help.


# Roll Call

I want to hear
everyone
on Earth
say their name,
at least once.
No one is allowed to die
until roll call
is taken.

# The Producer

Through bones of light
in the empty theater of space,
God jitterbugs.
We're actors stuck in New Haven,
cast in flops which fold during try-outs.
God smokes a plump Cuban cigar,
while perusing reviews at Sardi's,
over French champagne and pate.

We never get to the diamond lane of Broadway,
where God, a producer by now, rides in a limousine
holding an armful of red roses,
while resting his head on a pillow.
He raises the velvet collar of his overcoat
to cover his ears,
and then snuggles into the back seat
and points the chauffeur toward home.

God sinks into a deep sleep,
even though outside,
beyond the tinted window,
characters are being written out,
and buried underground
in full make-up and costume,
where they will remain
for the duration of the play—
dark spots on the lungs of the earth.

# Found Poem while Reading My Camera Manual

Unlike the combination
of the human eye and brain
that tries to overcome
a slightly out-of-focus picture,

the electronic rangefinder
looks for reality.

# Jailbirds

On Saturday mornings
I wore a lace undershirt
and fancy panties under my dress,
like I was getting ready for a date,
like I was dating Jesus.
Ginger snuck me into the chapel
to teach me how to be a Catholic,
I hated being Protestant.
All we did in Sunday school
was color pictures of Jesus with his lamb.
At the Catholic Church,
Ginger had holy water
to splash on her forehead.
She could bow and cross herself,
kneel and pray, confess her sins,
receive penance, whisper Hail Marys,
finger rosary beads and sob for forgiveness.
Ginger swallowed the blood and body of Christ
and chanted in Latin. All I got was milk and cookies.

If it were a race to God,
Ginger's church would win.
They had Christ hanging on the cross
with rusty nails driven into his hands and feet,
and tear-shaped droplets of blood oozing out.
His ribs protruded through slate-gray skin,
drained pale from losing blood,
delicate skin that hung in sad folds,
like a drape rippled over his ribs.
The Protestant church had plain white walls.
There was no life-size Christ writhing on the crucifix.

After praying in the chapel,
with holy water moistening our brows,
and after pummelling our hearts with our small fists,
we rollerskated down the hill to the candy store.
I liked the look of the candy store.
The chubby Sunday newspapers
stacked on the floor, the arts and leisure section,
the comics, the book review,
all but the front page news
which arrived in the middle of the night
when hopefully nothing else would change.
I liked to spin on the stools,
while biting the tips off wax bottles
then drinking the sugary lime-green syrup inside.
I liked to smell the hot fudge,
that the candy store man simmered
all day long in deep, narrow pots
with silver ladles sticking out of the lids.

Ginger and I studied the candy,
but we always bought a Milky Way and divided it in half.
I gobbled mine up,
but Ginger nibbled and savored hers.
I watched her eat,
so she always gave me some of hers.
I think because she was Catholic,
she knew how to take her time.

One Sunday night after dinner, my father was reading
the *Newark Evening News*
and he said, "Oh my God." And I said, "What?"
"Ginger's mother and father are in the newspaper."
I said, "Holy Smoke, why?"
The bigger the news the longer it took adults to spit it out.
He said, "Oh No." I said, "What?"
He said, "They were arrested." "For what?" I said.
"For stealing food from the A & P."
The next day in school,

children gathered in circles pointing at Ginger giggling,
shouting, "Jailbird, Jailbird. Your parents are jailbirds."
The kids were making a chant.
I went over to Ginger.
We sat down and I let my left thigh touch her right thigh
and I put my arm over her shoulder.
It was lunch time.
I looked at Ginger's face.
Her face was grimy from tears and sweat
and from wiping her eyes with dirty hands.
I unwrapped my sandwich,
which was roasted turkey on rye.
Ginger had bologna on white.
I didn't know what to say.
"My mother took the food to the car,
thinking my father had paid," she said.
"I'm sure," I said.

Ginger's parents were the first people
I ever knew who stole something.
Every time I said the Lord's prayer after that
and I got to the line,
"Give us this day our daily bread,"
I thought of Ginger's mother and father being arrested.
For years afterwards, I imagined them walking handcuffed
from the food store to the police car.
Two skinny kids, in their late twenties,
named Mr. and Mrs. Palmer
with four children waiting at home.


# The Roof Garden

An orderly wheels my mother to the roof garden
where cigarette smoke clings to the plastic chair,
and a roll or two of artificial turf
is worn thin from wheel chairs and heels grinding in.

The orderlies are relieved
to escape the psychiatric ward
where everyone talks at once,
which rocks with the choppy opera of the deranged.

As the patients mill around the roof garden,
it's clear they don't know what to do,
cooped up too long under neon lights that buzz all night.

Some of the patients wear clothes
donated by strangers
unmatched tops and bottoms.
Fred wears a gray cardigan over his pajamas.
He's upset about something.
My mother's wheelchair touches Fred's.
She takes his hand and strokes it.
Fred begins to cry.
My mother, who nursed her second husband John,
bedridden for years
places Fred's head on her shoulder,
leans her body in and says,
"There, there, John, everything is going to be all right."

The nurse in charge rushes over and snaps,
"Fred is not your husband,"
then wheels my mother
to the other side of the roof,
where she remains until the hour ends,
her head bowed,
her hands, like two embryos,
still in her lap.

That night in the dayroom *Titanic* is screened for the patients,
while Mary calls the governor,
Hilda looks for the hosiery department,
and Fred says, to no one in particular,
"We're all drowning on dry land."

# Alchemy

If we had to buy words
and could only use those we'd purchased,
I'd buy *beefy* and use it with *beefy* soul.
Or I'd buy *salt* and *ice* to use with blood.

If we could look at them before buying
as in a jeweler's case,
I would consider *"uncapped longings,"*
and I'd definitely buy *blue*,
and save it for something special,
perhaps a prayer book,
unless it conjured up images of pornography
as in a *blue* movie.

You always have to consider
how people might have used words,
before you buy them.

I'd buy *membrane*, just because.
*Icy, swollen* and *crisscrossed*
should be allowed to stay together, somehow,
as children dispersed by death or divorce
feel cold and discombobulated without the other.

Some words would cost more than others, of course,
the hard to find words, the rare words, the *blue* words.

The most valuable are those that are meant.

I saw Robert Haas at a poetry reading at UCLA.
He said one day one of his black students
burst into the classroom saying,
"I get it now. Jokes are the blues of the Jews."
I get it now. Poems are the blues of the people.

So much suffering being strummed
and blown and drummed into the earth.
So much pain, waiting for words to be turned into poems.

# Scrabble

I sit with my mother.
We play bingo and scrabble with the others.
I join in. We all laugh and talk.
I remember how she helped me make friends,
when I was a little girl.
Then the next day I go to the hospital
and she is depressed and confused, again.
Thinking I said I would be there at noon,
now at 4:00 she is feeling betrayed.
She talks to the nurse about flying off the roof,
because taking an overdose of pills
can have an "uncertain outcome."
"I don't want my daughter
to have to live through my death twice,"
she says, strangely considerate, even while hallucinating.

I give her the sugar-free ice cream
I brought for her,
and the pretzels filled with organic peanut butter,
and we sit in the hallway on 3 South,
a locked psychiatric ward,
and I put my arm around her
like we're a couple sitting at the movies.
We sit in silence while she eats her ice cream
with her head bent down.
We wait together
there in the neon hallway
for hope to return,
which here may appear
as a willingness to play bingo,
or as a desire to join the others
in the dining room for tea and ravioli.

# Dinner Party for Buddha

Incense burns, bell rings, Bill bows, sesshin begins.
Bill's milky white toes are splayed beneath the black robe
which dangles at his ankles.
His bare feet glide along the stone floor
which gleams like a lake
from the candlelight on the altar,
which is a plank of wood holding Buddha,
balanced on a dragon,
beside a purple orchid inserted into a clear vase
with pebbles at the bottom of the water.
Bill's sea-shell pink robe underneath the black one
produces a hint of color at his neck like a blush.
His hands form into a prayer position at the heart center.

We will sit facing a blank wall
from six in the morning until nine at night.
Most sit on round black zafus
placed in the middle of square zabutons.
We will sit like strange fishermen and women,
on private rafts,
casting out our lines
into the sea of wall.
If we hook thoughts
we reel them in to look at them.
Then, we throw them back,
even the big ones.
We resume counting.
Inhale one, exhale one, inhale two, exhale two
all the way to ten and back again.
Empty buckets, full buckets, spilling out, filling up.

I hear Elisabeth interviewing,
whispers at the entrance to the zendo.
Like a hymn, her voice creates a purr in my mind.
Dinner will be a ballet with bowls.
Oryoki.

Then more bows and bells.
After dinner Michael will lead us on a march
through the zendo to clean up.
Later Ray will scuttle
to be first in line to Bill's room.
Even though he lugs a chair
he beats us all to the interview line.
The oldest and the quickest.
From Bill's room I hear members deciphering koans.
Faint sounds like in a dream remembered.
People laughing, barking, mooing, talking, crying, howling.

Left hand cupped over right,
we walk like monks in the sun
and later like monks in the moon.
The skylight tells the time on the floor.
During kinhin I walked on the moon.
Our legs are sore and our lower backs ache.
Sesshin draws to an end.
We gather for dharma talk with the sangha.
Bill checks with Elisabeth to see if he can say
what he wants to say.
She is his tender censor.
She shakes her head and he winks.
We roar with laughter as he cracks a joke.
He's a zen monk with a hard hat and a tool belt.
Elisabeth is a flower.

Looking for Buddha nature finding Elisabeth, Bill,
the sangha and Marilyn pregnant with twins.
Looking for Buddha nature, finding love.
It's all an open secret someone said
inhale one, exhale one, inhale two, exhale two
all the way to ten and back again.

# Intensive Care

I'm like a stage mother,
getting my mother ready for viewing.
When the doctors make rounds
I stand by her bed.
To keep her case interesting
I talk twice as much
and use lots of gestures.
She's in a coma.
We're a team
auditioning for the doctors
to save her life.

# Marilyn's Ashes

I like hanging out with my mother
in 9 east at the end of the corridor,
even though she is in a coma.
The therapist massages her
while classical music plays
on the boombox I brought from home.
I sit here watching her breathe,
remembering how we were always broke when I was growing up.

At the mortuary in Santa Monica,
a counselor in a hot pink suit with black tights
leaves the room to okay a lower price with the funeral director.
She comes back with his offer.
It's like I'm buying a car.

So I go to another mortuary,
where my mother will be taken when she dies.
It's where Marilyn Monroe's ashes are kept.
My mother once told me
that Joe Dimaggio sent a dozen roses there every day.
She smiled when she told me,

pleased with such extravagance.
My mother always loved the larger-than-life.

# The Light Man

Every night after our last scene,
Jeffrey and I ran upstairs,
and laid on our bellies in the light room
to watch the play unfold below.
The star of the show wailed while his wife sobbed.
J.B. and Sarah lost all their children before the second act.
The character I played was killed in a car accident.
Jeffrey's character died in a war.
J.B. fell to his knees. Sarah screamed, "Curse God and die."
The light man changed the light.
I thought the actors had the most important job.
They bellowed and shook their fists.
They recited words of rage, words of forgiveness.
But when the play ended and the curtain dropped,
it was the light man who made the theater dark
so that no one could get up.

# Fear

Imprisoned
and tortured
by the Chinese
for a decade,
a Tibetan Buddhist nun
said that her biggest fear
came when she realized
she was in danger
of losing
her compassion
for the Chinese.

# Night Ends

Night ends,
but the dark seeps out,
from under the doorway,
shadows stain the day.

Still, I can't imagine
that heaven is more beautiful
than earth with all her scars.

**S**usan Salomon Neiman was born in Manhattan but has spent most of her adult life in Los Angeles where she currently resides with her husband, her two grandchildren and three dogs. She is a psychotherapist who also teaches writing workshops. She has taught nursery school and worked at a magazine and a publishing company. She has written six chapbooks and has been published in *California State Quarterly*, *Ship of Fools Press*, *Explorations*, *Satori*, *Poetry in the Garden*, *Blue Violin*, *Rockhurst Review*, *The Tmp Irregular*, *Urban Spaghetti*, *Poetry Motel*, *Spillway*, and *ONTHEBUS*.

Photo by Catherine Neiman

# Apartment 5A

My mother slept late each morning,
wrapped like a mummy in the sheets,
while my father and I ate breakfast together.
He hid behind the *New York Times*.
I ate looking at the silver candlesticks
or the flower pattern on my plate.
We went down the elevator in silence,
he to Wall Street,
and I to school.
My mother was never home when I returned.
The apartment was still.
A portrait of George Washington stared at me
from above my brother's unplayed piano.
The maid stayed in the kitchen
shining the candlesticks.
I crept around the empty rooms
feeling as if I might disappear
if no one held my hand.
I touched myself hoping to connect.

# When I Was Twelve

When I was twelve, I worried
about bombs falling when I tried to sleep.
Every plane I heard overhead
made my heart beat faster
and my stomach tighten up.
I worried I would fail the history test the next day.
I bit my nails and thought I was unpopular.
I wished I would get breasts like the other girls.
I wore an undershirt and they were wearing bras.
I thought I was stupid
because everyone else was so smart
and I couldn't understand geometry.

When I was twelve,
my mother embarrassed me.
She was not like other mothers.
She was prettier and walked
around the house naked
or wore my father's bathrobe and slippers.
My father criticized her at dinner,
asking her what she had done all day.
She would leave the table in tears.
I didn't want to be like her.
When I was twelve, I was scared that I would die
but I wanted to die.
I stared out our twelfth floor window
and thought
of somersaulting
to the pavement below.

# The Dance

I lie next to my father
while he sleeps beside me.
Our bodies do not touch
and I listen to his breathing,
turning towards his back
until I fall asleep.
In the morning
I feel shame
because I am not in my bed.
I tiptoe into my room
where my mother sleeps
next to the chair
with my uniform on it.
I dress in darkness
and eat breakfast in the sunshine
with my father who reads the paper.
Then we go our separate ways.

I to school
and he to Wall Street.
We do not reunite
until I tiptoe into my sleeping parents' bedroom
and tap my mother on the shoulder.
She goes to my room
and I join my father
in our night time dance,
where we do not speak
or open our eyes
or acknowledge its beginning
or its end.

# Family Dinner

My brother and I
place stiff white napkins on our laps,
knowing there's apricot souffle for dessert.
Candlelight flickers over the mahogany table.
My mother rings an engraved silver bell.
Clara arrives in a black uniform
with a white organdy apron,
carrying a silver platter
with leg of lamb and roasted potatoes
surrounded by a hedge of parsley.
She places it at the head of the table
in front of my father
wearing his blue silk smoking jacket.
She passes string beans, mint jelly and gravy.

He carves the pink flesh with surgical precision.
Then, pointing the knife at my mother,
he scolds her for how little she did that day.
She flees the table in tears.

My brother and I are quiet,
no longer wanting the souffle.
We are excused and go to our separate rooms.

Forty one years later,
emptiness blossoms inside of me,
an uninvited guest at my table.

# Love and Literature

I was sixteen the summer we drove across the country.
We started in New York
and ended in California.
The station wagon was loaded with teenagers.
Through most of Pennsylvania and Ohio
I read Jane Austen, how Emma Woodhouse misread
evidence and misled others.
I began *Jane Eyre* in Illinois
and read it through Iowa and South Dakota.
Jane was walking down the corridor of Thornfield Hall
when we crossed into Idaho.
Rochester hadn't appeared yet,
but I was caught up
by Jane's vision of a larger life
when suddenly the car flipped over
and landed in a ditch.
No one was hurt
but I had insomnia after that,
especially with the lunatic in the attic,
and took red seconals to sleep.
I started *Portrait of a Lady* in Wyoming,
where we stayed at a dude ranch.
Just about the time Madame Merle
introduced Isabel to Osmond,
I noticed how cute the cowboys were.
I stopped reading for awhile.
One night, a cowboy felt my breast

and stuck his tongue deep into my mouth.
I hated to leave,
but soon we were crossing into Montana
and I was sitting with Isabel in her dumb,
dark house of suffocation.
Most of the country after that
was a blur to me,
except for the Hoover Dam
which I remembered because it was so big
it held back enough water to fill an ocean.

# Marabou and Mahogany

Before she grew old Grandma used to stand on her head.
She was a *femme fatale,* a flapper
who danced all night, drank bootleg gin
and had three abortions on a kitchen table.
She was a beauty, dressed only in beige
and neglected her sons, I heard.
Grandma ate breakfast in bed.
Pink marabou feathers framed her face.
She fed the dachshunds bacon from her slender fingers.

Grandpa liked mahogany and English antiques.
His grandfather clock chimed every hour.
He preferred his dogs in the kennel.
When Grandpa died, Grandma sold the English antiques.
Everything now was pink and gold.
"Tacky," my mother said.
Grandma lay in her petal bed in her rose room
drinking gin and tonics.
Her false eyelashes were like those of llama, long and curling.
She applied each single lash one at a time.

She was either dozing or smoking
in her pink marabou bed jacket.
She talked to me of death, of curling up

in her black and gold Chinese chest with the dragon on top.
In her dreams, she dances the Charleston
and stands on her head perfectly,
neither arm trembling,
neither elbow caving in.

# Buddha in My Garden

Buddha watches me
as I peek through morning glories,
smiling as I weed
curling vines from his feet
that cover lotus legs.
A fluttering hummingbird
sucks white blossoms
from the kumquat tree
I touch sun-warmed stone.
His hands open.
My sweat drips
on his now bare lap.

He sits
contemplating tangerines growing,
crawling lizards,
swooping jays,
narcissus, wild indigo,
and golden koi undulating
under two water lilies
on still water.
Stone sunflower of my heart
seeing through closed eyes.

But white gardenias turn brown,
pansies shrivel,
goldfish die
and thorny vines cover Buddha.
I stub out my cigarette in a geranium pot

and fling it toward the dying ivy.
I hear leaf blowers roaring in the red smog heat.
Dust patterns the cracked glass table.
Buddha ignores my August despair.

# Birthday

Before I turned 54,
I thought of aches and pains,
needing glasses,
craving cigarettes,
lines around my eyes,
and my friend dying of cancer.
I could let myself sink
deeper and deeper in my bed.

Instead I gave a party,
dressed in white silk,
with gardenias in my hair
and mother of pearl from Bali
hanging from my ears.
I filled the house with rubrem lilies, chrysanthemums,
sun flowers and ginger,
lit beeswax candles
and danced the fox trot
in the humid night.
I ate couscous with apricots,
spring asparagus, baby lentils
and blew out candles on tarte tatin,
read my poetry, kissed and hugged
and opened gifts with purple ribbons.
(I only bummed one cigarette from the waiter.)

# The Japanese Restaurant

Five of us are eating dinner at a Japanese restaurant.
I mention an article I'd read in the Sunday papers
that 16th-century China was a good time to live.
After Yung-Lo reconstructed the Grand Canal
so ships could navigate inland,
he extended China's borders
beyond the Great Wall
and sent Cheng Ho, his loyal eunuch,
on sea expeditions
throughout the East, as far South as Africa.
"Actually," I say, correcting myself,
"that was the 15th century."
"Please pass the sushi,"
is the reply.
I feel like a child at a table full of adults.
It must be the acoustics,
I tell myself,
but then they laugh
and I hear something about quiche Lorraine,
lost keys and traffic on the Pacific Coast Highway.
I think of the debris scattered along the shore that morning;
broken styrofoam cups,
torn plastic bags among piles of gravel
and dolphins arching against a smoggy sky.
Someone says, "hub caps and epilepsy."
I remember my vacation
when I walked on a frozen lake
in the thick white crust of snow
and my foot sunk
piercing the coating of the lake.
When I pulled my boot out it was wet and dripping.
I screamed to my husband
and my grandson
far in the middle of the Lake.

They continued walking away.
Now at dinner,
I hang onto words
that dissolve in my tea like sugar.
I bite into the sushi
and crisp sweet vegetable tempura.
I want to join these people
and their conversation,
but instead I remember
the box turtle I saw sitting on the road,
how I'd stopped my car and picked it up,
marveling at the pattern on its shell,
and the way its legs and head retracted at my touch.
I placed it in the pond
and watched it burrow in the mud.
"Please pass the soy sauce,"
brings me back to the pale wood table
and the empty crumpled sugar packets
unfolding like flowers.

# Falling

The trick, she thought, is knowing how to fall.
Balance is temporary.
The dice are thrown and float
through the air like dandelion feathers.
She had been a tree, a half moon, a cobra and a dog.
Now she wanted to hold a bow and arrow
and aim straight for his third eye.
She didn't want to grab his cock
under the table or sleep with him
when her sheep in bear skin
was meeting with lawyers in lion suits.
She was bored with Neiman Marcus,
exfoliation and I Ching in the afternoon.
She wanted to play house with his chakras

under the glass roof of their igloo.
Her soul was a frozen popsicle
which made his tongue ache.
She was a Venus Flytrap
and he was her fly.
Dressed in a platinum helmet,
studded with diamonds,
she cried tears of coal
which ignited on the Fourth of July.
Her face was destroyed
and in her despair,
she became a mountain.
The plastic surgeon said,
"Nothing can be done."

# The Deer

Brown marbles stare at me from a dead deer,
lying among pine cones and pine needles.
I am pierced with sorrow by the thought
that I am a human being.
The goddamn hunters drive by
in their red pick-up truck,
wearing plaid shirts and baseball caps.
"Fuck you," I shout,
but they don't hear me.
My hike is interrupted
by the rat-ta-tat of rifles.
The killers, the My Lai massacrers
have invaded my woods.
I must return to the place
behind a fence where ginger wilts,
calla lilies cry tears of terror,
and blinking fireflies mistake
fireworks for friends.
A calico cat creeps behind the rhubarb,

waiting for unwary rodents.
A snake eyes me without blinking
and I think of the deer and leap across the lawn
like Isadora Duncan.
Then strangle on the treachery
in my throat and vomit yesterday's yearnings,
which lie tarnished on the dry grass.
I am empty
and shatter like a broken goblet,
sparkling in the sun,
but useless.

# Ending

In the plum blossom shadows,
I feel the chasm of his indifference.
Like a deserted beach at dawn,
when the moon has gone
and the sun has not risen,
the sand has only the ocean
for company.
I remember marriage vows,
and hands held in childbirth.
He no longer hears me.
Pastels fade to black and white.
I no longer see him.
He, who was once my bones
is only a symbol
in my dreams.

# Chiseled Stone

I have been a woman who screams,
breaks crystal wine glasses on a red tile floor.
I have torn off his glasses as he was driving,

twisting their metal frames
and throwing them out the window
so he couldn't see my black tears.
I have been scared to be alone,
fearing if I couldn't see myself
reflected back in someone's eyes,
I would disintegrate into little balls
of mercury scattering to the corners of the room.
I have scratched my arms until they've bled,
walked in circles in the night
and hidden under the covers in the day.
I have tried to numb myself
with pot and Quaaludes, LSD and cocaine.
I've stood on a window ledge
and leapt like a deer into another galaxy.
I have raised two children,
married three men,
written words in squid's ink
and saved them
in chiseled stone books,
bound in crimson.


# Crossing the Street

I sit outside drinking coffee,
a breeze blowing my hair forward.
I've been reading over my old poems
and feel as if I'm in a trance,
as if my poems were dreams
and I am dreaming them again.
I float towards my mother.
I am thirty, grimacing in childbirth.
I am twenty-one, walking down the aisle, my arm linked with
    Father's.
I am fifteen, dancing the foxtrot with my boyfriend.
I am six, learning to read in a green primer.

I am three, wetting my pants at nursery school.
I am two, having a temper tantrum because my stuffed rabbit is
    being washed.
I am one, learning to walk into my nanny's proud arms.
Blast off! I explode from my mother's womb in a gush of water,
red and wrinkled, a purple birthmark over my left eye.
Then the sounds of traffic bring me back to this wrought iron
    table,
my feet on the ground,
my thoughts circling backwards and forward.
A black dachshund sits on a blonde woman's lap,
and a man in shorts with crutches is at the table next to me.
I drink my coffee until only the dregs remain
and shiver as I walk to the corner,
and cross the street where there is no light,
hoping the cars will stop for me.

# White Lies

Spiders are crawling in the bathtub.
I wash them down the drain
and fill the tub.
Then lower my body into warm water
and worry about the spiders.
Was I wrong to kill them?
Should I have cupped them in my hand
and let them out the window instead?
I think about the small murders
I commit every day of this new millennium.
The ants I step on,
the white lies I tell,
the way I pick at my cuticles,
and tell myself I'm no good.
I watch the water swirl down the drain
in a clockwise direction.

# Too Late

for the three-legged dog,
for the ants marching on the counter,
for the hawk circling in the sky,
for the dishes sitting in the sink,
for the man with his teeth in the glass,
too late for the sparrow that flew into the window,
for the spider without a web.

Too late for the gas bill,
for the manilla folder,
full of unopened envelopes
from Neiman Marcus, the bank,
the tax man, the shrinks,
the L.A. Mission, the Indian children,
the Sierra Club
and the Department of Water and Power.
But I'd rather lie next to him
and let him bury himself in me.
It's never too late for that.

# Ordinary Things

My daughter and I are staying in a cabin on the Big Sur Coast.
She sleeps in the twin bed by the window
dreaming her dreams,
I sit on my bed writing poems,
then put on my sweater
and walk across the lawn,
black in the moonlight,
to the pay phone at the Lodge
and call my husband who will not be home.
Then I will go to sleep
and my daughter will wake me
and tell me I'm snoring
and I will say, "I'm sorry"
and go back to sleep

and start snoring and she will wake me again.
In the next room, someone is taking a shower
and outside my window, I hear a waterfall.
The shower stops,
but the waterfall is constant.
The shadow on the page in the shape of my hand
is constant too
as is the sleep of my daughter in her bed.
Soon I will sleep,
dreaming dreams
I may
or may not
Remember.

# The Green Pen

The green pen explodes in my hands
leaving emerald blotches on my skin.
Earlier I'd debated whether to use the red pen or the green.
I think of Lady Macbeth saying,
*"Will all great Neptune's ocean wash this blood*
*clean from my hand?*
*No; this my hand will rather*
*the multitudinous seas incarnadine,*
*making the green one red."*
So I go to the bathroom and start scrubbing,
rubbing and rubbing with soap.
The water turns green,
but still the stain remains
like the stain of a childhood
that refuses to fade.
My heart pounds.
My face flushes hot and cold.
I toss and turn in sleep.
Then wake unable to think,
unable to breathe.
I look at my hands.

I am no longer four years old.
On my ring finger is a red circle,
a ring of rash.
Now I smooth Neosporin over the spot
as a lover would rub lotion into a loved one's shoulder.
The veins in my hands rise like pale green rivers
and my skin ripples like the surface of a lake on a windy
     afternoon.
Later on that day my friend spots the green on my thumb
"You have a green thumb," she says,
 and I laugh,
 I laugh.

**C**aron Perkal was born in Los Angeles, California and grew up in Pacific Palisades. She graduated from Art Center College of Design in Pasadena, and received her bachelor's degree in fine arts. She currently works in Los Angeles as a freelance art director in advertising. Throughout her life she has enjoyed painting as well as writing. In 1996 she enrolled in a workshop and began writing poetry. She has done readings in several venues throughout Los Angeles.

Photo by Ron Derhacopian

# At the Poetry Reading

The boy siting next to me
says he hopes he is killed by a tiger, a shark or a snake.
He says he loves animals and he hopes he is killed by one.
He asks, " Do you like any sort of reptiles?"
"Lizards" I say.
"Yes," he says, "I am going to get an iguana.
If you have two of them you'd better have an outdoor cage."

On the other side of me a woman strokes her husband's neck.
She combs her fingers through the ends of his freshly cut hair
and onto the back of his neck.
She keeps doing it over and over again.
It makes a pleasing, scratching, thumping,
rustling leaves-with-a-rake sound.
I feel every curl of her finger, every tickle at his neck.
I remember what it was like to be so familiar.
So coupled.
So married.
Knowing you were going home to Sunday's paper
and the *TV Guide,*
the queen-size bed and the spooning of ice cream
into bowls and eaten in front of TV.
I am homesick.
I keep getting homesick.
My stomach cries out *I want to go home.*
Like a mantra it pulses from my shoulders.
Bleeds from my chest.
I don't know how to answer it.
I don't know where home is.
I haven't known for a very long time.
I never made one. I am an adult with no home.

The boy next to me says,
"My father will go insane if he reads the poem he brought."
His father reads.
He does not go insane.

When the boy leaves I tell him, "I hope you get your wish.
That one day you are killed by a tiger, a shark or a snake.
That one day you are killed by the animals you love so much."

# I Lost My Innocence to You

I wonder what you would have done
if you had known that I would be
the only girl you would ever kiss.
Just your stupid cousin.
Two kids experimenting,
one summer day,
while the family
wasn't looking.
Open-eyed and close-mouthed
underwater—
the taste of chlorine
the only memory of our passion.

I wonder what we would have done that day,
bobbing underneath the shadow of the diving board
trying to hide what we were doing from your father,
if we had known that before the year had ended
the death that we had seen
in shoot-'em-ups and monster flicks
would come to you by fire.

# The Ember of Sorrows

There are places where I trip,
places where I fall
into my mothers arms
and land safely.
But most of the time when I stumble
it is not that easy to recover
from the bruise that begins to form on my life.

Like a blue-black reminder
of what things could have been
a butterfly lands on my knee
and pumps its wings up and down,
fanning the ember of sorrows I let go of long ago.
Threads of silk are woven into beautiful robes
even in the land
where a million Chinese babies cry.
And a beetle rubs its legs together
and creates a breathtaking song
even in the land where famine takes children from their mothers.
A three-year-old boy gulps for air
while his brother clings to their mother
in a melting trailer
that burns from front to back.
They are all found together, huddled in the bedroom.
Two boys,
a mother,
and a mother's mother
all found their death
in the arms of those
who were supposed to protect them
from the fall.

# Every Day I Wonder, "What Is He Learning Now?"

I return from the funeral
with a picture of Johnny in my hand.
I hold my hand over one side of his face
and then the other,
see if I can find an answer there.
One side shows anger.
The other dissappointment.
For three days now
I have taken out the picture and examined it.

One side of his nose is longer than the other.
I think about his face.
How much flesh is left?
I turn the card over.
Birth date.
Death date.
I have read the whole story.
I know the end.
I see him on the quad in high school,
long coat,
smile,
confident walk.
I see him talking to me six months ago.
long coat,
cane,
gray ponytail.
He is disappointed.
I am angry.
We are living.
Johnny barracaded himself in his bedroom.
Typed out a suicide note.
He made a list of who he wanted at his funeral.
What he wanted them to say.
He laid himself on his bed.
Did he fold his hands?


# Shower

It is my job
to help my grandmother shower.
I live in an upstairs apartment in her building
so I come down every Sunday
while her brother is out playing golf
and stand outside the shower, watching...
waiting for a fall, guarding against disaster,
as if my tiny frame could be of any help.

I hold her hand and help her balance
while the mist that bounces from her body wets my clothes.
I watch her run the soap over her now protruding stomach,
wrinkles forming smile after smile from her belly to her pelvis.
A few fine hairs all that are left to cover her pelvic bone.
I watch her clean the cavern where her left breast used to be.
Suds fall across the brown and yellow hollow
down to the thighs that formed a lap for me
to bounce on as a girl.
Blue veins bulge behind her knees.
Purple lines run down her legs in crazy squiggles
as if a child has been naughty with a magic marker.
There are lumps and bumps and everything is ugly.

When her shower's over  and it is time for drying.
I take a fuzzy pink towel from the rack and cover her.
I manuever her carefully across the tiles
to the safe carpet of the bedroom
where she sits at her vanity while I brush her hair.
She stetches out her leg and turns her ankle
then she says, "Can you believe
these were voted once the best legs at Stanford?"

# A Place that Was Good

Colorado was a place that was good.
Always good.
My husband and I, we were good in Colorado.
Things were good, with the snow and the rain
and the trout fishing we did.
I can see him.
See him in the truck asking for my help.
I see his face in the rear view mirror as I stand outside.
He wants me to direct him,
show him the way,
so he can back himself up to the hitch on the trailer.
I know we will fight,

and he'll tease,
he'll say I can never direct him correctly.
It is a good kind of fight.
The kind that brings us together
and gives us things to laugh about as we watch bugs
gather on the screen of our trailer,
attracted by the light inside.
I can see the red rock behind us turn black
as the sun makes its way
down toward the ground.
We cook
and he drinks beer
and I let him
and I am not mad.
I am happy to be with my husband
in the trailer,
with the bugs and the bed that we make from the couch,
and the loud sound of the air conditioner above us.

"You know that I love you,"
he said to me at Green River
next to his truck on Valentine's Day.
Green River,
where we pulled out the lawn chairs and the canopy
and laughed that we were going to turn into fat-rumped
trailer park people.
We loved it,
loved being young and talking with the others about our rig.
The older people.
They would admire our rig.
They would want to see how the canopy worked.
They would ask how much it cost.
They were impressed by our youth
and our twenty two foot little honey
and we would never tell them,
tell them that we were rich
and we could be taking my father-in-law's jet to Colorado.
But we loved the trailer.

So we took the trailer
that we had bought at Travel Town in Orange County.
The trailer we had picked out together,
had chosen over Airstreams and much bigger get ups.

I loved my husband so much then.
I loved his smell
and his voice, too deep for his size.
I cannot remember his face anymore—not a face
that I knew for twelve years.
I can remember his breath and the feel of his hand
inside of mine, the soft skin
of his feet on top of mine in bed,
"Cowboy boots keep them soft,"
that's what he'd say.
I can remember his knees.
The way there were patches with no hair
inside his knees.
"Rubbed off by horses,"
that's what he'd say.
"Horseback riding,
that's why I've got no hair there."
I remember how he protected me
from dogs in the hills of Topanga,
shot at imaginary Indians on the cliffs,
as he showed me where he went to Boy Scout Camp.

I've trained myself to hate him.
It's the only way I can survive.
I picture him doing all of these things with his new wife
and I want to call him.
I want to somehow stop it.
I want him to be mine again.
I want to laugh with him and camp with him.
I want to feel his stomach against the small of my back.
But I will never feel these things again.
They are gone.
As gone as the trailer I sold last summer.

# Pets

He calls to tell her that he found a bird,
an exotic gray creature that landed on his driveway.
He brings it to her house,
shows her the way it likes to perch on his shoulder.
He calls the bird 'honey'
and shows her the way it comes to him.
She watches him looking at the bird,
she sees him take it home.
He buys it a cage.
feeds the bird,
becomes attached to it.
She hears the bird sing when she goes to visit him.
When they talk on the phone
the bird chirps in the background.
She has given up her dog
so that she does not have to leave his house
to go home to feed it.
She goes home to nothing.
He comes home to the bird,
that free creature that landed on his driveway.


# In the Highlands

Her body flowered with fingertip bruises,
she hears him call her "C"
from the unlit bedroom down the hall.
She looks in the bathroom mirror
as she feels the stream of urine join the wet
that is already between her legs.
And as her lover shifts,
as her parents sleep in each others' arms,
thinking that their daughter is good,
attending school,
making a future for herself,

she looks at her cheeks in the mirror
and smiles at the redness, the rosy glow
that has made this man—
the man that calls her "C,"
the man that she cannot tear herself away from
even as he beats her in the cool darkness
of his underground garage.
Even as he flips through her history book,
tearing out the pages that she has shared with him
and stuffs them in her mouth,
causing her to choke and gag
Even as he calls her Sue
or Angie
or sometimes even Cunt
she runs to his bed and his face, his jaw lit by the moon.
She longs for the sound of pebbles
that he will throw against her window
sometime after midnight,
sometime after the bars have all closed
and she is the only one that waits for him
and the pleasure of his freckles
under her fingertips
under her wet, anxious tongue.

# Love Notes

He loved me despite the manila folders
that we had kept on each other,
noting each defect,
recording every fault.
I had made a notation on December 15th 1983:
*appendix scar,*
*6",*
*light purple.*
In August of '85 I had taken out the folder again
and slipped in postcards that he had sent me from France,

I had to correct his spelling three times.
Out fell a paper I had stuffed in the folder
sometime in '82:
*Not sure if I like his smell,*
*car used to belong to his sister,*
*has been in love before,*
*too shy.*

When we were breaking up, I did what I'd never done before,
I looked in the folder he had on me.
He had scrawled some things in black ink,
other things were typed.
*And I don't know if I was supposed to talk about lipstick*
*Sept. '84,*
was the first thing I read.
So he didn't like my lipstick.
What was wrong with it?
Too pink? Too red?
Rubbed off too soon?

Then I realized he was talking about a fight we had had.
I had accused him of being too feminine.
He was making notes on himself,
places where he had gone wrong.
*Talked about my old girlfriend*
*Forgot to call and tell her I was going to be late*
*Wore that shirt she hated*
His folder was full of regrets.
Mine was full of criticisms.


# Red

Red
Red
Red rock
Lots of it
Glorious

Beautiful
The air
I can breathe the air
Clearly
His hand
His face
Next to me
I swear I feel it
He doesn't have to touch me
I am happy
There is red rock
There is beauty
And I feel him
He is with me
He's not leaving
No he's staying
He is never leaving
We are camping
There are eagles
It is summer
It is winter
There's his hand again
It is in mine
He is happy
We are happy
We are we
We're never parting
He is staying
We are camping
He is watching
I am cooking just for him
I am living
It is now
Only now
There is no yesterday
There is Sunday
Only Sunday

Yes—it's now it's not tomorrow
I am happy
I'm not writing
We are living
We are living


# Past Present

She tells me
she is writing about things
that just happened
and that this is her problem.
I push at my eggs
and look at the ring
the orange juice has left on the table.
I have written so many poems
about things
that happened so long ago.
Things that I might have forgotten.
Like the time
that I first saw a piece of you naked.
The width of your back
a surprise.
Like the gift of ballet shoes
wrapped neatly in tissue
at Christmas.


# Souvenirs

There are thick August nights
when the whole family loads into my father's Burgundy MG.
My brother and I straddle the stick shift
balancing between our parent's seats.
I am forever next to father.
I watch him comb his hair in the rear view mirror,

his thin aluminum comb leaving its teethmarks
in perfect rows through his shiny black head.
My mother double knots her white
or sometimes aqua
chiffon scarf,
because, of course, on summer nights
the MG's top is ever down.
As we make it up the hill towards Baskin Robbins,
dreaming of Baseball Nut and Chocolate Ribbon
the speed blows our faces into smiles.

There are turquoise days spent together at the beach,
my brother always in the ocean,
my father always pacing back and forth
across the shoreline
his feet drumming the hard wet sand as he yells,
"Ricky, Ricky you need to come in now."
A thousand boys turn their heads
fearing they too will soon be called
to their blankets and their mothers.
We eat sandwiches spiked with sand
and have a snapshot day while my father paces.
Once we're home starfish boil in a pot on the kitchen stove,
stiffen into souvenirs.
In the yard my brother and I run naked
while my mother turns the hose on us.
This is so much better than a shower.

# Mary

It is my birthday
I receive a gift in the mail
from the mother I just met.
She signs the card "Mary."
These days, this Mary
does not forget my birthday
even though she told me

the first time we spoke,
the first day she admitted that she knew me,
that honestly,
she could not remember the day
I was born.
She could not remember
the day I was pulled
from her body, bloody
and crying to go home.
She does not know the color of my eyes,
she does not know my name.
She only knows what she was told by nurses,
the doctor
and her husband
who made her take a vow
that they would never, ever
talk about this day again.

# While at the Manicurist

The woman feels the need to share with me.
Tell me what it is to be a mother.
Such large woes.
The widening of her pelvis.
The spread of her feet.
The way the baby's collar bone snapped
when she gave birth because it was such a tight squeeze.
She tells me about the responsibility
the women take in organizing the schools.
The men are of no use, she says,
then she excuses them:
They have their work.
She glances at my left hand.
I know what she is searching for.
She pretends I have not caught her in the act.
I have already told her I have no children.

But she wants to know, do I have a husband?
Are children a possibility?

# First Date

They talk of God
and push boiled red potatoes around their plates.
Her silver fork sharp and her tongue silent
when he says he is okay with having no children,
that this must be for him, God's will.
She thinks of God
and will
and the times she laid herself down on a table, aqua blue,
the times she watched a doctor's head between her legs
as life was pulled from her,
as God's will was packed up, bloody,
in a plastic bag and hauled to some trash can,
somewhere in an alley,
in a lab,
in a place where will does not exist.

# White Room

We sit in my bedroom.
Our tiny feet make dents like questions
in the white poplin bedspread my mother traded
for the blue chip stamps she and I licked and collected
in books kept in our already too-full kitchen drawer.
Suzan and I are both seven,
born two days apart.
We flip through pages of *Life* magazine
run our hands across photographs of transparent stomachs,
pink babies like brine shrimp
curled and sucking their thumbs.
The Miracle of Birth,

the unfolding of life,
recorded for the first time
through the miracle of x-ray photography.

Suzan has three older sisters
and she knows much more about sex than I.
So when we read that the baby was a mistake
I ask Suzan what that means.
I knew how babies were born.
A man rolled on top of a woman,
inserted his penis into her vagina,
an act so repulsive and intentional
I could not imagine how this could happen by mistake.
"A man and a woman are like magnets,"
Suzan explains.
"They cannot help but be pulled toward each other."
I imagine the horror of this thing.
A man being pulled to me
no matter how far away I lay from him in bed.
Was there no way out?
"Even if you are wearing underwear?" I ask.
Oh, that is of no help.

And until I meet Eugene I don't really know what she means.
The drives up canyons.
The need to strip off our clothes.
My breast caught under the steering wheel,
his tongue reaching into me.
My mother angry,
warning me not to spend hours in his parked car
in front of our house.
She is afraid of what the neighbors will think.
I am not afraid of neighbors or babies made by mistake
I cannot help but lose my virginity to this boy and his hands,
his mishaven face rough against my cheek.
I do not care how he treats me, the way he flirts with other girls.
I care about his tongue, his fingers,
his flesh smooth as a porpoise against my own.

**E**laine R. Warick is a retired medical writer/editor who lives in Los Angeles with her husband, Lawrence, a psychiatrist. Together they have written articles on the Norwegian artist Edvard Munch which have appeared in *Psychoanalytic Perspective on Art* and *The Journal of the American Academy of Psychoanalysis*. Elaine is the author of a book of poems and short stories, *Like A Hind Let Loose*, and a recent chapbook, *Lova's Alley*. Her material has also appeared in *The Los Angeles Times* and *The Saturday Review of Literature*. Elaine received her degree in English Literature from UCLA.

Photo by Bob Perin

# Huntress

I stand next to my father
in the desert.
He is a big man wearing levis, boots,
a flannel shirt and brown leather jacket.
A baseball cap covers his blue-black hair.
He holds a rifle:
"Look through the sight,
aim at the rabbit,
and pull the trigger.
That's all there is to it."
My brother shoots first
and misses.
The frightened rabbit runs
through the desert brush,
the three of us
in pursuit.
I am next.
I take careful aim
and shoot.
The rifle
kicks me back.
I got the rabbit.
I look away when my father
picks it up
by its hind legs
and holds it high in the air.
"Fried rabbit tonight,"
he says.

Years later, my brother tells me,
"I missed on purpose."
"And I pleased Dad," I tell him.

# Mrs. King

Kingy was my nanny
when I was six years old.
We lived at the Grand Canyon
where my father was a Major
in the U.S. Cavalry.

Kingy was a widow
and a retired waitress.
Before she came to work for our family,
she had been a Harvey girl
at the Bright Angel Lodge
in the Grand Canyon.

When she wasn't living with us,
she lived alone in a clapboard cottage
down the road from our house.
She had a chicken coop and a lilac tree
in her backyard.

Kingy had gray hair pulled into a bun.
She wore black dresses
with little pastel flower prints.
I used to help her order them
from the Sears and Roebuck-catalog.

My parents traveled a lot
so it was Kingy who read to me,
who played the piano and taught me songs,
who showed me how to tie my shoes,
braid my hair,
embroider pillow cases.

I thought she loved me
because her own daughter
died of tuberculosis
at age six.

One Christmas,
when my parents were on a trip,
Kingy brought a miniature Christmas tree
into my bedroom.
It was decorated with satin bows,
red and green glass balls
and strands of tinsel.

I knew my Jewish mother
would be very angry
if she found out about the tree.
When she came back,
sometime in the New Year,
she asked me about the tinsel
I had hidden under a book on my play table.
I said, "I don't know how it got there."
It was the first of many lies
I would tell her
throughout my life.

# Figs

> *"Every man under his vine and under his fig tree."*
> *I Kings 5:5*

Some biblical scholars
say it was the fig
Eve ate in Paradise,
not the apple.
Pictures of Adam and Eve
fleeing the Garden of Eden
show their naked bodies
covered with fig leaves.

I think of this as I pick
four fresh figs from a basket
at Vicente Foods in Brentwood.

It is the end of August—
time for the fig harvest.

I ate my first fig
when I was eight years old.
A pear-shaped fruit,
brownish, purple on the outside,
pink flesh on the inside,
filled with hundreds of tiny seeds.
I picked it from a fig tree
growing on the Goldwater Ranch
in South Phoenix.
I sat on the grass
next to the red brick wall
eating the sweet fig
and drinking cold milk.
Two English Spaniels
playing a few feet away
began to copulate.
I kept eating my fig.

I learned to dive that summer,
first the low board,
next the high dive.
Diving in the desert,
eating milk and honey,
watching dogs procreate—
All so biblical.

# Camping

It was just the two of us fishing for trout
up there in those White Mountains.
Dad pumped the water out of the well
and all these thin hairlike worms
were swimming in the pail.
He poured the water

through his white handkerchief
into a thermos
and said it was okay.

That afternoon
crossing Clear Lake
my horse tossed
me forward and backward.
My father held the reins high,
showing me how to guide the horse,
but my horse started swimming
away from the bank.
Dad hollered at me
to pull the reins
one way or another
but I couldn't
and Dad had to pull me to shore.

Today I am making rainbow trout
in orange sauce.
I just rinsed the fish
and patted it in flour.
I poured the olive oil
into the black wrought iron skillet
and when it was hot
I put the fish in
and stood there a minute
watching it fry.
Then I fingered the leather cord
hanging around the
end of the spatula,
shoved the spatula into the pan,
and guided the fish
through the river of oil.

# Movie Show

Twelve years old.
Sitting on a stool at the lunch counter
in the Greyhound Bus Station
in Phoenix, Arizona.
Meatloaf, mashed potatoes and gravy—
the best I've ever eaten.
Across the counter a small, skinny
man takes a seat
and stares at me.
I look away from him
and order lemon meringue pie
for dessert.
When I finish I leave the depot
and walk up Central Avenue.
I pass Goldwater's Department Store,
turn on Washington,
walk by the Navajos
sitting on the sidewalk selling
turquoise and silver jewelry.
They are wearing velvet on a hot day.
I'm wearing a yellow pique sundress
and white sandals.
The Strand Theater,
in a forbidden part of town.
Eddie Cantor in a triple feature,
*Kid Millions, Strike Me Pink,* and *Whoopee!*
A large box of popcorn,
a seat in the center,
the place is almost empty.
I'm watching the first
of ten cartoons when the man
comes down the row
and sits right next to me.
I ignore him.
I feel his hand on my breast.

I move to one side and he
touches me again.
I leave.
Walk through the lobby
to another entrance
and reenter the theater taking
a seat in the back row.
I watch the man, his silhouette
in front of the flashing cartoon.
He looks around, then leaves.
I wait, but he does
not come back.
I look at the screen
and see Popeye
swallow a can of spinach.

# Aunt Ann (April, 1944)

I was taken from my home in Phoenix
to stay in Kansas City.
I wanted to go back to Arizona
but my Aunt Ann was dying of cancer.
My mother sat in a rocking chair,
staring into space,
saying nothing.

Flakes swirled in the new chill,
Missouri so cold and damp.
For the tenth time
I trudged the boulevard
and the neighborhood with my sled,
like Santa Claus at Christmastime
and fell, skinning my nose
on the iced sidewalk—
trying to catch
a street car—It didn't come
so I waited there

next to the movie theater
playing *Blossoms in the Dust*.

A month,
then two and a half,
then four months...
counting over the winter.
My mother a vegetable.
God, a silent snow.

# Blood Sister

It was a hot afternoon in Phoenix, Arizona.
The four of us gathered
around the kitchen stove.
Hubert, half Chippewa on his mother's side,
was shirtless and his skin glistened
on his hairless chest.
His wife Louise, a full-blooded Chipewa,
waited with me for the ceremony to begin.

Hubert held the embroidery needle
over the gas flame
until the tip was glowing red
then pricked the inside of my brother's thumb.
A small drop of blood formed.
My four-year-old brother's eyes opened wide.
Hubert stuck the needle into his own thumb
and when he started to bleed
he rubbed my brother's thumb and his together.
"Now we are blood brothers," Hubert said,
"And you are a member of the Chippewa Nation."

When it was over I asked Hubert
if I could be his "blood sister."
"No," he said, "Girls don't do this."
I started crying, but Louise said,

"We'll start a hope chest for you,
   for when you get married,
   that's what Indian girls do."

Hubert built a cedar chest
that he put at the end of my bed.
Louise bought linen tea cloths
and ironed flowered patterns on them
for me to embroider.

Seven years later,
with the hope chest full,
I married my first husband.
He was a hairless man just like Hubert.
Although the marriage ended in five years,
I still have the hope chest in the garage,
filled with old *Arizona Highway* magazines.


# Madeleine

Madeleine was French.
She came to Arizona
after World War II
and worked for us as a housekeeper.
She taught me how to draw.
One day I drew a green frog
on a yellow lily pad,
and Madeleine Scotch-taped
it to the bathroom wall.
When my father came home
he ripped it off the pink enamel,
scolding us for making a mark
on the fresh paint.

When my mother and father
left for a trip
Madeleine moved her boyfriend

into the house.
She made elaborate meals.
We sat at the dining room table,
set with Wedgewood china
and Waterford crystal glasses.
She even lit candles.
We sat like a family
eating Madeleine's French food.

She taught me how to make gravy.
She called it *roux*.
We put a stick of butter in a pan,
melted it, then added flour,
salt and pepper.
I stirred the mixture with a big wooden spoon
until it turned brown.
Then, Madeleine poured milk in the pan,
whisking it into a smooth sauce.
We ate it that same afternoon
over buttermilk biscuits.

When my parents came back early
my mother fired Madeleine
because there were over a dozen
white cotton sheets
stuffed in a closet,
washed
but not ironed.
I know it wasn't about using the good china
because I never did tell her.

# Snakes

When I was a girl,
my father and I climbed a hill
near a Hopi Indian pueblo
in northern Arizona.

When we got to the top,
my father said, "We can't let anyone see us,"
so we crawled on all fours
to the edge of the mesa,
lay down on our bellies
and wiggled like combat soldiers
until we could look into the canyon below.

I saw six men,
their bodies covered
with reddish-brown paint,
dancing in a circle
with live rattlesnakes
in their mouths.
They were wearing leather loin cloths
and fringed moccasins.
They had red and white feather headresses.
Some other men were following the snake dancers,
chanting and waving yellow feather wands.

We watched them for about ten minutes,
the August sun searing at our backs,
then my father tugged at my shirt
to pull me away from the edge.
When I was far enough back
I stood up and tried to brush the dirt off me.
My father said,
"That was part of a secret Hopi
ceremony that white men are forbidden to see.
Don't tell anyone about this,
not even your mother."

Hiking back across the desert,
there was a cloudburst.
I thought we were going to drown.
We ran up a hill from a wash
just seconds before it turned
into a raging river.

I thought the Hopi Spirits
were punishing
us for watching the secret ceremony.

When I got home,
my boots were caked with mud,
and my clothes were soggy and dirty.
My mother was angry when she saw us.
"I guess you and your father
have been on one of your hikes," she said.
"We were looking for rocks,"
he told my mother.

That night I dreamed
I was trapped in a cave
with rattlesnakes crawling toward me.
My mother woke me up
and asked me why I was screaming in my sleep.
I told her I was being attacked by rocks.

# Dinner at Bubba's

My Aunt Ann was in Menorah Hospital
dying of cancer.
My mother, brother and I
had come from Arizona to Kansas City
to say good-bye.

It was Friday night.
My mother's family
were speaking Yiddish
throughout the meal.
I didn't understand what they were saying
but I knew everyone was upset
because they were crying.
The candles were still burning
on the dining room table

when the family left
for services at the synagogue.

They left me to babysit
my two-year-old brother.
I was eight.
When he was asleep
I started clearing the table,
taking the dishes, silver and glassware
into the kitchen.
I washed and dried everything
and put them away
in the cupboards and drawers.

When the family returned
several hours later
my Grandmother went into the kitchen
and started wailing.
I watched her grab the silverware
from the drawer
and run into the backyard.
She plunged the knives,
forks and spoons into the dirt
beneath the cherry tree.

"Go upstairs," my uncle said.
"What did I do wrong?" I asked.
"You put the meat utensils in the milk drawer,
  now Bubba has to make them Kosher again.

I climbed to the second floor bedroom
and into the bed
where my brother was asleep.
I pushed him to the edge,
then shoved him over the side.
He hit the hardwood floor
with a thud.

In moments he was screaming.
My mother rushed into the room.
She grabbed me
by my shoulders
and shook me,
demanding to know what happened.
"I don't know," I said,
"He just fell out of bed."


# Mother

And she is young again.
Dressed in green silk,
her hair golden red,
skin white, eyes
watery blue.
She is slipping
over the edge of the cliff
into the mud.
I hear her screams,
but I cannot save her.
I try but I'm lost
on the mountain path
and not even Red,
the park ranger,
can get me on course
or pull my mother
from the Grand Canyon.

The squirrel
still digs for pinon nuts
and the tourist takes a picture
while my mother falls
down the gorge
into the Colorado.

# Dinner at Grandpa's

My Russian grandfather,
wearing a white Cossack shirt,
black pants and boots,
chases a chicken
across his backyard.
I am standing near the smoke house
when he grabs the chicken
by the neck
and swings it around
his head
screaming something in Russian.
The chicken is squawking,
its feathers flying.
Next, he slams the chicken
on a wooden block
and chops its head off
with an axe.
Blood sprays over the grass.
I wet my pants.
I feel the warm urine
dribbling down the inside of my leg.
Grandfather looks at me and smiles.
He announces in English,
"Tonight we eat
chicken and dumplings."

**V**icki Whicker grew up in a surfing town on the east coast of Florida and in a small Illinois town on the Mississippi River. After college she moved to a ski resort in Colorado, five years later she moved to the California coast where she lives with her eight-year-old son. As a fashion designer, she traveled the world to gather ideas and to work with the international factories. Currently, she is a commercial artist representative as well as a painter and writer.

Photo by Lou Bustamante

# Caught before Flight

Sun is sparkling on blue water,
a summer thunderstorm is moving in.
I still have that picture tucked inside a dusty red photo-album.
I stand with my father on the dock in front of a dark lake,
behind us the people of summer drift in their boats.

My father holds my waist as we pose,
his straight arm keeping a distance between us.
I tilt my head away from him,
let the breeze play with my hair.
My hands, two white doves before flight,
are caught in front of my waist.

He wears faded jeans and oil-stained boat shoes.
I go barefoot, in denim cutoffs,
new breasts melded into a ruffled tube top.
Over his left shoulder, two teenage boys,
in a white and red speed boat, grin like wolves
at my abundance.

My father's face is captured in a stiff grin—
he can no longer cover me up with guilt,
with clothing, with his eyes.
He is my chauffeur; this is my summer of love.

Flowers on my tube top fade into my skin,
clouds in the sky frame our heads,
I look into the camera and smile.
Summer begins.

Days spent skinny-dipping with boys in secret coves,
water running off our bodies
as we pull ourselves into boats
to make out in the silent heat of the afternoons.

Nights filled with stars pasted into the distant sky.
Beer kisses from a dark-haired boy in the back of a boat
rocked by our struggles; a blonde-haired boy's

desperate fingers in my bikini
as my father snores in our cabin under the trees.

The storm comes on the eve of the fifth of July,
heat lightning first, torrential rain by morning.
Leaves drop into the lake with the weight of the wind.
Father and I leave in the dark
with the car's heater at full blast.
We race in silence down slick back roads
towards home,
as if with so much speed
he could leave behind
what I had found.

# House-keepers

My neighbors' mom painted her lips
into a red joker smile,
smoked hard-pack Winston's
and drove a Mustang with rusted out floorboards.
Her daughters and I would watch tar and gravel
sweep by our feet
when the Joker gave us rides.

Their dad was an ex-Navy man
with a bad hip,
who, through open windows,
cursed God and his family,
every night, "Goddamn fucking sailors,
keep your fucking hands
off the quarter-deck!" he'd yell.
On ordinary summer days
their parents were not home
and I would lie on the white-flecked
linoleum floor of the girls' bedroom
and move my legs
to find the cools spots

underneath the bed.
Stacks of comics and dust bunnies
covered the floor
where the girls and I
would flip through our paper dreams:
Archie. Josie and the Pussycats.
Wonder-Woman.

When we were bored
we'd look at their mother's collection
of dried fish-eyes
in a cedar box.
Huge spiders watched us
from the corners of the house,
"House-keepers."
the Joker called the spiders,
"They're good luck." she said.

Their parents' bedroom door
was always closed
and we were forbidden
to enter that room
but we'd sneak in there anyway
because it was air-conditioned.
We'd sit on the bed without talking
and play paper dolls,
then we'd lie on the bed,
hold each other,
and try not to get up and run
as our chests hammered like woodpeckers.
After awhile we'd burst out of the door
into the heat and gulp the heavy air.
Happy to be kids.
Happy to be alive.

# When I Was Seventeen

When I was seventeen
my bedroom window
faced eternity
I watched rolling hills
fade into purple.
I watched tractors,
like primary colored insects,
plow rows of dirt
until dirt and tractor
disappeared into the horizon.

I wrote in my diary
and waited for my boyfriend
all day in that room,
surrounded by
red, white and blue
wallpaper flowers.

At dusk
I went down to the barn
to do my chores.
Buckets of oats
and fresh water
for my horses.
I sat on straw,
listened to them chew
and stamp their hooves
until another noise
caught my ear.

It was Jim
calling my name,
"Vicki"
"Vicki"
"Vicki!"

He must have found
the kitchen door open
and the TV-room empty.
He must have run up the stairs
to my room and found my diary open,
found the words that I'd written
at the end of that long day,

"In every love affair
there is the one
who loves the most
and that one is me."

I could hear Jim calling me
in a voice I'd never heard.
When he rolled the barn door back
and found me waiting,
he was crying.

The next day I wrote in my diary,

"In every love affair
there is the one
who loves most
and I will never forget
the terrible power
of being the one
who is loved the most."

# Undone Button

I am thinking of Lieutenant Button
The fighter pilot who crashed his jet
Into New York Mountain
Near Vail Colorado

Blue and white
He added the red
The missing color

Now he is frozen
And gone
And all for the memory
Of a kiss

A kiss is just a kiss
Until it eats your brain away
And you get those feelings
Kill
Kill
Be killed

And if
Mr. Button sir
You remembered a girl
Who took your body
Over a beer
And the hill

Well
I think I remember you Button
You blew through me one Vail winter
I took you to bed
It was just for fun
And I forgot you
I did
You came
I went

And you
Well
You weren't the first
(Or the last)

So Button
Why come undone
Over a memory

Was this memory more callous
Than the life you chose

A bomber
A killer for the Red
White and Blue

I think about my summers
After that winter
And count the men in between
Our night and you cashing it in

To blot out a memory
You challenge a peak

Can I satisfy myself
Over your dead body

I am aware
Of the small part I play
In this life
I bleed oil onto snow
Mixed with three parts
Of your blood
We melt together
And our fumes fly

Still
I cannot forget you
Soldier man
Or the piece of you I stole long ago
But you lost me
Button
When you found that
Mountain

# Snake Street Alley, Hong Kong

Always this
I belong in this city of dust and death
I am finally home

An old whore walking up ancient terraces
Between beggars and businessmen
Donkey dicks and deer pricks in jars
Baby pigs strung upside down
And drained of life
With leather hides
Like the insides of old wounds
Blood in the windows
Blood in the streets
I don't need to look at the faces
That pass
I know who they are
When I look at their buildings
Rust running down
Water and offal
Green slime dripping below
Shattered air-conditioners
Windows strung with grimy underwear
Hanging like flags of defeat
Over a pox riddled nation
Garbage rains down on my head
Like water from a Seagull's beak
I walk the city and smell the death
That has been following me all my life
Thin stream of death
Opened up now
Like a thundercloud
Filling my nose
Filling my head
I breathe deeply
Walk
Snake Street Alley
Up long stairs
Between an open-air barber and his client
And a rheumy-eyed man
Selling rusted knives and porcelain jars
With sex scenes etched into them

I stop and touch the various positions
Painted onto the bottom of the small bowls
Thin flesh-colored lines
Accented by dark scratches
Of pubic hair
And pin dot eyes
For the wedding night
The old man tells me
Gift to teach the bride
All of the positions
His smile is yellow and broken
And I think of a bride who does not know
All of the positions
As I step over World War II relics
Spread on a dirty cloth
Manned by another
Smiling toothless yellow man
How does it happen I wonder
As my twat itches in the afternoon humidity
The marble bathtub at the Hotel Vic
Was cool against my ass this morning
As I shoved the mobile shower head
Up against my pubic bone
And then down
Up and down
I thought of all the waiters
in New York City
And the bellboys
At Le Parker Meridian
Called out the name
Of my last lover
Imagined his head buried between my legs
As I arched my back
My ears underwater
The water pounding
And always
Alone like this

Coming to the applause
Of water pounding
A hollow song

In a hotel bathroom


# Ghuang Zhou, China

My Chinese driver
Heaves a sigh
As the traffic slows down
In the city
I ride alone
In the back seat
Of a factory owner's Mercedes
I lean my head against the window
And watch the rush-hour traffic

Men standing in a rusted bus
Sway like bamboo stalks
Brakes screech
Mopeds putter
Horns honk
Truck beds rattle
Dust swirls in the humidity
A black butterfly floats
Above the chaos

Yesterday
The red taxi I took to the factory
Had its own noises
It leaked exhaust
I sat next to the driver
As he played
Thread-the-needle
And beat-the-clock

Through the city
There was no seat belt

Today
A hot wind blows dust
Outside my tinted window
Canvas tarps fly
Motorcycle jockeys play
Their dangerous games
Inside this air-conditioned
Rich man's car
I remember that
I am an American
And I want to go home

# The Housewife-Poet's Scene

There she is
With the coffee
Always the coffee
Bitter
And so much to drink
And drink it she must
After all she paid for it
And to be a poet
Is to be frugal
To mourn for money
As it slips away
On two-dollar cups of coffee

The coffee is important
It sits in judgment
Of the journal
Of the poems
Of the chicken scratch
And demented doodles
Before it

See the tiny poet's house she lives in
A cluttered
Awful
Falling down house
The one with the neglected yard
It is the house
Of an old maid
Or an eccentric
The type of house
That neighbors
Whisper about
And small children
Gravitate to

And inside
There is that oven
That siren
That silent seductress
Enamel goddess
Barely used for frozen things
Yet patient as the expanding universe
Wise as a shaman
Always singing
In a pitch that only dogs
And housewife poets can hear

Now meet the small boy
Who does live there
The son who tells her
Mommy we can go to the park
And you can write poetry there
I won't bother you
He plays the understanding five-year-old
To her struggle
So well
Like a pro
Without
The judgment of the coffee

Or the anticipation
Of that oven

# Pushing 7½, Falling into 8

Tonight we lie on his bed
And he cries
I'm ugly
I try to hold him
Try to rock him
But he is all new
With his long arms
And hairy legs
And I find
That at seven-and-a-half
There is nothing small
Left for me
To comfort
He turns away
And cries from a place so deep
That there is no sound
Until the pain reaches his throat
And he says
Mama
I don't want to be me
I want to be a baby again

Does it matter
That he doesn't listen
To me anymore

Before bed he looked into the mirror
At the two teeth
Pushing from his lower gum
Crowding the wobbly baby teeth
That refuse to leave
I told him

You are so handsome
No I'm not he said
As he stared at the rows of tiny teeth
But you are I said
Mama he replied
I can see

Tonight when I try to hold him
My tear drops into his ear
What was that he asks
His dog curled at the foot of his bed
Lifts its head
The cat stands up
And stretches her long body
All three are unaware
That I am falling off the edge
Of this bed
That there is no room
For me anymore
And that this is new to me
This falling

# Raining Roses

My grandmother died
with rolled-down nylons,
like flesh colored mufflers,
around her swollen ankles.
She waited out her last days,
dark hairs growing longer
on her jutting chin,
blue eyes watery behind thick black
horn-rimmed frames, her frail head
covered with fluffy silver hair.

Her husband died picking her a bouquet
from their rose garden.

The roses taller than her,
standing over him,
their heads waving in the sun,
like pink, yellow and red
ghosts of her happiness.
Japanese beetles working
their oil green cases into the dirt,
undertakers searching for the gold
surely buried in their garden.

Grandfather was handsome until the end,
silver hair and gentle smile,
wicked sense of humor.
A Christian man, slim, dressed in plaids
and old faded denim, leather brogues
covered with garden dust.
Farmer. Gentleman.

She was in her room, dark and musky.
Days passing, stacked on top of each other
like the white bibles she used to keep on her nightstand.
Her ankles swollen, until one day she could only die.

I carry on alone in my small house.
My ankles trim, no nylons ever.
Just the family name and a longing for a love
that causes me to stay inside stacking days,
like bibles I have never read.

Today, I visited my rose garden—
white roses, green bushes, shorter than me by half,
and I picked all of the floppy white heads
with their faint scent, tore all the white petals
from their pale yellow centers,
then tossed them over my head to catch the wind
and shower down around me.
I did this with all the roses that were in bloom,
left only the buds.

I used to go to dark bars with young boys,
make out in the corners, pretend that I was okay.
But that is not going to work anymore.
I know that I am not okay,
especially when it's raining,
raining roses,
all over me.

For more than thirty years James Doolin's work has been shown in solo and group exhibitions throughout the United States and Australia, most recently a solo exhibition at the San Jose Museum of Art and the Koplin Gallery in Los Angeles, with whom he has shown since 1984. Doolin was a recipient of the prestigious Guggenheim Foundation Fellowship in 1980, three grants from the National Endowment for the Arts, and a City of Los Angeles Cultural Affairs Department Grant. His urban landscapes are tour maps of the soul that teeter on the edge of destruction, as if the end of the world were too beautiful a sight to turn away from. If Dante were alive today, he would swoon at Doolin's parallel images in *Twilight*—the white headlights on the infinite freeways of Los Angeles, souls destined for Paradise, and the red tailights headed in the other direction.

Lucinda Luvaas's work is shown nationally and abroad. Her work is represented by Leigh Hamilton, Santa Monica, CA, Pascal/Robinson, Houston, TX, and Space 12 Gallery, Boston, MA. She has exhibited in museums and universities in New York, California, Pennsylvania, and New Jersey, and Arkansas. Although her primary medium is oil painting, she creates work in varied media including electronic music, video, gouache, acrylic, monotype, etching, painted wall sculpture, casein, and murals. Her work has been the subject of magazine features and television specials. She has taught studio painting and mural painting workshops in California and New York. Currently, she is the Director/Curator of Mt. San Jacinto College's Fine Art Gallery in Riverside County, California.

# BOMBSHELTER PRESS

## Anthologies

**13 Los Angeles Poets** (160 pp.) $13.95

**Moving Pictures: Nine Los Angeles Poets** (62 pp) $5.00

**Raising the Roof: Poets Supporting Habitat for Humanity, Riverside** (72 pp) $10.00

**News from Inside** (39 Los Angeles Poets) (64 pp) $7.95

**The New Los Angeles Poets** (203 pp) $12.50

**Two-Woman Show (Haft/Laumeister)** (62 pp) $10.00

**After I Fall (Alexander/Kulikov/Lee/Wilson)** (64 pp) $8.95

## Books by Single Authors

**A Lone Black Gull (Michael Andrews)** (320 pp) $18.00

**Coffin Lumber (Michael Andrews)** (128 pp) $12.00

**Breaking Down the Surface of the World (Jack Grapes)** (62 pp) $10.00

**Lucky Finds (Jack Grapes)** (45 cards) $12.50

**Passion & Shadow (Judi Kaufman)** (98 pp) $18.00

**Crossing the Double Yellow Line (Stellasue Lee)** (95 pp) $12.95

**Corpses of Angels (Henry Morro)** (72 pp) $12.95

**Arrival (Doraine Poretz)** (78 pp) $10.00

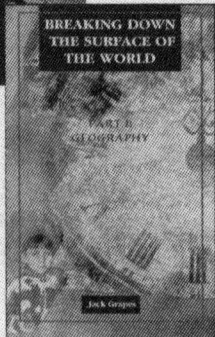

# ONTHEBUS

**Double Issue 6/7** (330 pp.) $13.50
Charles Bukowski letters; interviews with David Mura & Joyce Carol Oates; provocative photo-essay by Penny Wolin, "The Jews of Wyoming."

**Double Issue 8/9** (330 pp.) $13.50
Interviews with Allison Lurie, Anne Waldman, Thomas McGrath, Ai; color portfolio with poems by Pablo Picasso and surrealist paintings of his lover, Alicia Rahon.

**Double Issue 10/11** (350 pp.) $13.50
Frida Kahlo full-color portrait & essay; last journals of Bukowski; interviews with Thylias Moss & Alice Notley; translations of Pablo Neruda.

**Issue 12** (265 pp.) $11.00
Bukowski journals & photographs; interviews with Sharon Olds & Grace Paley; essay by Jack Grapes on the painting of F. Scott Hess.

**Issue 13** (265 pp.) $11.00
Interviews with James Dickey & Tom Wolfe; Bukowski album of journals and poems.

**Issue 14** (312 pp.) $11.00
Art by Susan Manders & Ruth Bavetta; Bukowski journals & poems; work by William Stafford, Ai, Donald Hall, Sam Hamill.

**Double Issue Issue 15/16** (324 pp) $15.00
Art by Ruth Bavetta & Susan Manders; Bukowski journals, letters, poems; interviews with Annie Dillard, Dorianne Laux, Kim Addonizio; drawings by Mindy Alper & Matt Wardell; work by Richard Jones, Lyn Lifshin, Ai, Suzanne Lummis, Katharine Harer, Kate Braverman, Charles H. Webb.

**www.bombshelterpress.com**
**BOMBSHELTER PRESS**
PO Box 481266 Bicentennial Station
Los Angeles CA 90048

www.ingramcontent.com/pod-product-compliance
Lightning Source LLC
LaVergne TN
LVHW011224080426
835509LV00005B/301